TOP MARIJUANA STOCKS FOR BEGINNERS

HOW TO INVEST IN BIG STOCK MARKET PLAYS

RANDALL STEWART

TheStewartEdge

CONTENTS

DISCLAIMER

As stipulated by law, I cannot and do not make any guarantees about your ability to get results or earn any money from the ideas, information, tools or strategies presented.

The risk of loss in trading securities and options can be substantial. Please consider all relevant risk factors, including your own personal financial situation, before investing or trading. Stocks and options do involve risk and are not suitable for all investors.

Use caution and always consult your accountant, lawyer or professional advisor before acting on this or any information related to a lifestyle change or your finances.

Past results of any individual trader or trading system published by the author are not indicative of future returns by that trader or system and are not indicative of future returns which may be realized by you.

All strategies and examples are provided for informational and educational purposes only and should not be construed as investment advice under any circumstances. Such set-ups are not solicitations of any order to buy or sell a financial security.

Any financial numbers referenced here should not be considered average earnings, exact earnings or promises for actual or future performance.

∼

INTRODUCTION

You've heard all the hype about the cannabis industry. Many advocates are saying that it's the next best thing to happen to the pharmaceutical industry since sliced bread, butter and jam arrived in the food industry over 90 years ago.

When I was knee-high to a grasshopper, toast played a major part in my elementary school education. It was a simple, quick, easy-to-prepare meal for sleepy-headed, late risers; not to mention that it tasted delicious. Sliced bread was a game-changer. As is cannabis, in changing the pharmaceutical and healthcare industries.

There's no better time to get in at the ground level of the cannabis industry than right now. The North American market in 2017 was conservatively estimated to be a $10 billion industry. Fast forward to 2023 and many experts are expecting it to grow to at least $35 billion.

Introduction

Global growth in the industry is expected to be exponential as opposed to linear with projections placing the market at $63.5 billion by 2024. This is fantastic news for the investor looking to grow their investment portfolios significantly while the industry expands over the next 5 years.

Being a young industry, there's huge growth potential over the next decade as major players expand their footprint across the globe. Expect to see phenomenal growth in the industry when the U.S. legalizes cannabis on a federal level. It's only a question of time before this happens as global pressure is mounting to remove marijuana from the list of Schedule 1 dangerous drugs that have been deemed to have no potential therapeutic value.

Investment opportunities abound in related industries who'll either team up with cannabis producers or provide needed equipment, products and services in order for the cannabis industry to continue growing.

For you, the investor, most cannabis stocks are relatively inexpensive versus stocks in more mature industries. This is a huge advantage in the early years of stock investing as less capital is needed in order to control a significant number of shares.

Most big cannabis companies also trade options on the stock. By controlling blocks of shares of those stocks that trade in the options market, you can create an attractive monthly income stream. Options trading is beyond the scope of this particular book. However, if you would like to explore how you could generate a relatively passive stream of income from essentially renting out your stock each month, check out my guide "Covered Calls Beginner's Guide".

Institutional investors see the long-term growth potential for the industry as being favorable. Positive momentum is on your side when it comes to anticipated growth in the overall industry over the next 5 years.

However, not all investment opportunities are good ones. Before we have you investing your hard-earned money in any opportunity, you'll want to have a deep understanding about how the cannabis industry makes its money and what constitutes as being a good investment.

You're toast without knowing the basics about the industry and what to expect from it. Burnt and unbuttered, I may add.

So, what can you expect to learn by the end of this particular guide?

This resource is founded on current best practices in stock investment, along with the latest developments and research into cannabis use and production. We're seeing rapid change in this growing industry with new insights into what it can and cannot do. Technological advances into the production and processing of cannabis are allowing a plethora of cannabinoid-rich products to enter the global market.

But with so much information out in the markets, how do you wade through all the hype surrounding the industry to make the right educated decisions? It's like having to shoot pool with a wet rope. Sheesh!

While wracking my little hamster brain, I came to the conclusion that you'll benefit the most from "actionable" insights. You'll quickly discover that this resource focuses on "how to" get things done - from finding and selecting market leaders to timing when to enter and exit specific stock positions.

You'll also discover why marijuana is so special as a medicinal plant. More specifically, I'll address some of the ailments currently being treated with cannabis derivatives. By seeing what the big picture has to hold for the healthcare industry, you'll be in the enviable position of knowing which companies could benefit significantly as medicinal marijuana becomes more mainstream.

The second section of the book delves into the exciting world of stock investing as a do-it-yourself investor. All of the material presented in this section has been tried and tested. You'll pick up sage advice from an assortment of industry leaders.

You'll be introduced to the F.A.S.T. approach to accelerating your wealth. The acronym F.A.S.T. stands for FINDING potential stocks, ASSESSING their growth potential, STRATEGIZING which investment plays generate consistent returns, and TIMING when to best enter and exit positions.

You'll discover which 10 trends in the marketplace you can capitalize on for years to come.

To save you time and a bottle of Tylenol, I'll provide you with a detailed overview of 20 potential stock investments that you could place on a watchlist to explore. These are some of the best marijuana stocks to consider investing in as the industry grows exponentially on a global scale.

You'll learn how to invest in those momentum stocks poised to explode on the stock market scene. To do so, we'll look at just a handful of fundamental and technical indicators that'll make the decision-making process that much easier.

We'll delve into how to profit from volatility in the markets. And contrary to what you may have heard, you'll learn how to better time entering and exiting the stock market so as to optimize your profitability.

By the end of this book, you'll have a deeper understanding as to how you could profit from the cannabis industry with a small investment of your time. Imagine spending just a few hours each week creating a tax-free income stream. Wouldn't that get you as excited as a clam at high tide?

My fervent wish is that you'll find something in this book that's going to resonate with you and make a significant difference in your life. I know that cannabis has opened up many doors for me from coping better with health challenges, to appreciating the finer things in life and tapping into my creative side more often than not.

Ready to see what's so special about cannabis?

~

1

WHAT'S SO SPECIAL ABOUT CANNABIS?

Before actually looking at various marijuana-related stocks that you could potentially invest in, you'll need to have a basic understanding as to how the cannabis industry is set up. By knowing what consumers could potentially be spending money on, you'll be in a better position to find profitable investments. This section sets the tone. By the time you finish reading this chapter, you'll have an in-depth knowledge of why cannabis is such a good investment opportunity.

Why is cannabis so desirable?

The reason why cannabis has gained international attention is that it contains more than 200 different cannabinoids, of which at least 60 have promising medicinal and therapeutic capabilities. Cannabinoids are found mostly in glandular trichomes, which appear on floral clusters or buds of the plant. They're also located on those leaves coming in close contact with these clusters or buds.

Cannabis also contains 30 terpenes of note, which combine with cannabinoids in ways that affect how the cannabinoids are being absorbed and used by the body. This is precisely why the man-made, THC-based pharmaceutical "Dronabinol" shows so many negative side effects and doesn't work as well as cannabis in its natural form. No current synthetic drug can replace what Mother Nature has so generously created to heal and rejuvenate the body.

And what are terpenes you may ask? They're aromatic chemical compounds found in all plants, such as flowers, fruits and vegetables. Terpenes are very volatile and fragrant, giving marijuana it's strong odors of pine, citrus, diesel, sour, etc. They play an important role in interacting with cannabinoids to produce subtle variations in the medicinal effects of each plant. Our understanding as to how all of these chemicals interact in the body is growing as research continues in this area.

The two most talked-about cannabinoids are THC (tetrahydrocannabinol) and CBD (cannabidiol). THC is known for its ability to quickly act on the brain producing a psychoactive response. Varieties rich in THC tend to be mood-stimulating. You may have heard about it being recommended for daytime use. CBD typically produces a calming effect on the entire body, as opposed to the typical "head high" with THC-dominant varieties. CBD-dominant varieties tend to be more sedative and relaxing and are often recommended for nighttime use.

I should point out that cannabinoids are present in all parts of the cannabis plant. The highest concentrations can be found in the mature buds, with lower concentrations in the seeds, leaves and roots. Ripe, resin-coated female flowers or buds is what is most highly prized from any medical grow.

What makes cannabis so special is found in the resin. When an unpollinated female plant or "sinsemilla" seedless plant develops, the bulbous trichomes located on the flowers produce the highly, sought-after resin. This resin contains all that steamy goodness we want to help cure what ails us.

Trichomes evolved as a means for the plant to defend itself from pests and to help with the dispersal of pollen. The bulbous trichomes situated at the top of the plant in the flower clusters secrete cannabinoids, terpenes and fats as a sticky resin. Being delicate, they can easily rupture releasing terpenes that give the plant its distinctive odor. Once ruptured the cannabinoids are quickly oxidized losing their medicinal value. When the buds are harvested at their peak ripeness, carefully manicured and allowed to dry they contain the highest concentrations of medicine.

Why such a fuss over CBD?

Over the past decade, we've seen a shift in interest as to the myriad of medicinal benefits that CBD and other lesser-known cannabinoids possess. Celebrities like actor Morgan Freeman, singer Olivia Newton-John, actor Patrick Stewart, and singer Melissa Etheridge have all publicly proclaimed the benefits of cannabis. Each of these individuals suffers from ailments that cannabis has helped.

Actor Matt Damon has gone on the record as saying:

> *"The first time I smoked was at home with my mother and stepfather; they were like, 'If you're going to do this, we'd rather you did this with us.'"*

Very progressive parents, wouldn't you say?

Our understanding of how CBD interacts with the body in addressing pain, seizures, tremors, hunger, and mood is growing and so is the movement towards producing more CBD-rich cannabis varieties. More cultivars are now looking at growing more CBD-rich crops to meet the growing demand for CBD-related products.

Until recently, CBD was primarily sold as hemp oil. Hemp contains very low concentrations of THC (less than 0.3%) and small amounts of CBD (usually less than 4%). Grown on an industrial scale, enough "hemp oil" can be extracted from the plants to be used primarily for topical applications and in edible products.

In my opinion, a better-quality source of CBD comes from Cannabis Indica plants that are grown for their higher concentrations of CBD. Some varieties can produce concentrations as high as 20%. Cannabinoids sourced this way increases the number of sought-after, medicinal components that can be used to produce a myriad of cannabinoid-rich products.

We're discovering that those CBD-rich varieties that also contain appreciable levels of THC are able to mitigate pain better than either cannabinoid on its own. This is one reason why, you may be best served by products produced from Cannabis Indica varieties, as opposed to Cannabis Sativa (hemp).

What's the Government's take on marijuana?

During the alcohol prohibition era in the 1930's, the US government began regulating cannabis. It was outright banned in 1937 with the Marijuana Tax Act. And in 1970 it was classified as a "Schedule 1" drug, which meant that it was deemed to have no medicinal benefits. Marijuana could no longer be grown and studied, unless Federal approval was granted. Cannabis went from being touted as having healing qualities and being a safe and effective medicine prior to 1937 to being banned as a dangerous narcotic without the scientific evidence to support the claim. Confused? This makes as much sense as head-butting a cactus, wouldn't you agree?

In 1964, the tipping point for the modern era of cannabis research occurred in Israel when tetrahydrocannabinol (THC) was isolated. Since then countries around the world have identified dozens of beneficial and promising compounds in the plant. Fortunately, with this greater wisdom comes greater acceptance globally.

Despite opposition at the federal level, a growing number of states have legalized medical marijuana. Thirty-nine states have legalized medical marijuana as of 2021.

The most significant development to occur on an international level was the legalization of recreational marijuana in Canada on October 17, 2018. From an investment perspective this development has set the global stage for massive international growth of the industry. Mexico is slated to follow suit in decriminalizing marijuana and recognizing the medicinal benefits of this life-giving plant.

What's so alarming is the U.S. Federal Government's refusal to acknowledge the health benefits of medicinal marijuana. The Federal Government continues to threaten U.S. citizens who use cannabis with criminal charges.

Former U.S .President Barrack Obama has admitted that:

"The war on drugs has been an utter failure. We need to rethink and decriminalize our marijuana laws."

Gadzooks! Government is supposed to work towards supporting the collective good of the nation and not suppress life-saving research or denying individuals access to medicine shown to improve the quality of life.

The Canadian federal government has sent a clear message to the rest of the world that the legalization and decriminalization of cannabis is the future. Extensive research can finally be conducted as to how we can receive the optimal benefits from this incredible plant.

Both U.S. and Canadian research companies have set up shop in Canada to do just that. This means that in just a few years' time Canada will be at the forefront of doing cutting edge research into the benefits of this wonderful plant.

Imagine the investment opportunities that'll abound as a result. Who knows, in a few years' time, we may see new Canadian cannabis strains like Justin Tru-dope, Celine De Bong, Sask-hash-ewan or Marijuan-eh? popping up across North America.

Is cannabis safe?

According to comedian Barry Crimmins:

"Marijuana is a very dangerous drug. Some people smoke it just once and go directly into politics."

As actor-comedian Bill Murray so succinctly puts it:

"I find it quite ironic that the most dangerous thing about weed is getting caught with it."

Interestingly, there have been no reported deaths attributed specifically to a cannabis overdose. The worst-case scenario for most users who over-indulge is that they'll pass out and possibly wake up in panic mode with a headache, dry mouth and being hungrier than a bear coming out of hibernation looking for a bag of Doritos.

As with any medication, consultation with an experienced medical professional should be one's first course of action before indulging. The challenge is finding a healthcare professional who has the training and experience with cannabis. Unfortunately, most medical professionals lack the formal training to be able to offer up-to-date advice. The majority of universities do not currently provide their med students with an appropriate grounding in the medicinal benefits of cannabis.

Of greatest concern are potential interactions with other prescription drugs you may be taking. For example, CBD can inhibit enzyme activity of cytochrome P450 in the liver, which the body uses to metabolize certain prescription medications. Consulting your local pharmacist may help guide you in avoiding any adverse effects and getting the most out of your prescription meds. Be aware that cannabis products containing THC increase the effects of alcohol, Valium, and codeine. Avoid mixing the two, especially if you intend on getting behind the wheel.

There's a growing trend of Americans who are using cannabis in their retirement. The elderly or those new to cannabis may express a concern when using THC-rich products for the first time. The psychoactive effect may be alarming or uncomfortable. In general, you'll see a higher number of negative side effects with THC than CBD, which is a "non-intoxicating" cannabinoid.

Did you know that If the whole world smoked a joint at the same time, there would be world peace for at least two hours, followed by a global food shortage? Yes, consuming cannabis products can leave you raiding the kitchen cupboards afterwards. Restraint may be the best course of action. For example, should you eat too much pasta, you could end up with a pot belly.

The most common negative side effects of using cannabis are dry mouth, itchy eyes, feelings of paranoia, being anxious, headaches and light-headedness. Depending on the variety you're using you may experience some of these less-desirable effects. The worst side effect of marijuana is watching 40 minutes of The Simpsons and realizing that you've seen the episode in question seven times before.

The negative side effects that some people experience are going to be minor and easy to address. Unlike many pharmaceuticals, cannabis is one of the safest medicines to use for a host of illnesses and health challenges. As singer-songwriter Melissa Etheridge, puts it:

> "Instead of taking 5 or 6 prescriptions, I decided to go a natural route and smoke marijuana."

Unlike opioid overdoses, cannabis does not cause respiratory depression resulting in death. In fact, those who use cannabis to manage pain often reduce or eliminate their need to use prescription pain killers.

In the following chapter we'll take a look at how cannabis is consumed. Once you understand how marijuana can be processed and used, you'll be in a better position to see which cannabis-related industries have growth potential from an investment perspective.

~

2

WHAT CANNABIS PRODUCTS ARE AVAILABLE?

Knowing what products consumers are willing to spend money on, opens up the possibilities of finding companies that we can invest in through the stock market. Before we delve into what stocks to buy, here's an overview of the most popular ways that cannabis can be consumed. I've broken them down into three general product categories:

1. Inhalable.
2. Edible.
3. Topical.

But before we explore the pros and cons of each category of consumption, let's take a quick look at how cannabis can be processed to create a concentrate that can then be used in multiple applications.

Concentrates have several distinct advantages over just dried bud. They are a purer form of cannabis that contains very little vegetative matter. Being concentrated, you'll require less product to create a desired effect. Processing often results in a product that is cleaner and easier to store long-term. Also, concentrates are versatile in that they can be inhaled, ingested or applied to the skin depending on their end use.

When the dried buds are converted into a more concentrated form, this usually involves separating the vegetative matter from the cannabinoid-rich resin that coats the buds and those leaves located close to the buds. This can be done with technologies that involve butane, carbon dioxide or barometric chambers.

The future of cannabis is in the purification of the raw organic material into clean concentrates that can be used in a variety of applications. Cannabis extracts are easier to ship around the globe and easier to quantify as to cannabinoid and terpene levels when compared to raw bud.

1. Inhalable Products:

The most common means of using cannabis is to either smoke or vape it. The cannabinoids in dried bud can be converted from their acidic "inactive" form to their decarboxylated "active" form through the mechanics of smoking or vaping. Whether you're smoking or vaping, cannabinoids enter the bloodstream very quickly through the lungs. The effects of your dosing will be felt within minutes.

Since smoking or vaping is a rapid delivery method, you can easily learn how to control your dosage by simply inhaling one dose at a time and waiting two to three minutes between doses. Once you have a base level established, future dosage becomes that much easier to regulate.

Inhalable products can be loosely grouped into three categories, namely smoking, dabbing and vaping.

(a) Smoking:

Smoking cannabis buds is currently the most common way of getting the cannabinoids into your body. It generally doesn't require any sophisticated equipment, just cigarette paper or a pipe, some crushed bud and a lighter.

Unfortunately, since you're burning the buds, not only do you inhale the cannabinoids but you're also taking in other toxic chemicals, such as hydrogen cyanide, carbon monoxide, tars, and a host of polycyclic aromatic compounds that are known carcinogens. Another downside is that smoking tends to waste a lot more bud compared to other methods of inhalation.

One-hitter cannabis pipes are becoming more popular amongst daily users. These inexpensive, easy-to-use pipes can deliver a controlled dose for those who wish to smoke cannabis to treat their health condition.

(b) Dabbing:

Dabbing is the process of heating a small quantity of hash or concentrate using a heated "nail" made of titanium, ceramic or quartz along with a water pipe or bong. The "nail" device is usually heated with a butane blowtorch until red hot, then a dab of concentrate is placed on the nail. This flash-melts and boils the concentrate generating a vapor that can be inhaled. Since inhaling the air that's been superheated can burn respiratory tissue, most dabbers cool the vapor through a glass or silicon water pipe.

As you can surmise, most cannabis users shy away from dabbing. Most people don't care for the elaborate set-up required for traditional dabbing. For most daily users of cannabis dabbing is not a viable means of self-medicating, especially when out in public. To address this concern, compact handheld units are coming out into the market that use electrical heat to vaporize the concentrate.

The advantage of dabbing is that you can inhale concentrated quantities of cannabinoids with less toxic smoke compared to smoking dried bud. These extracts can reach 80% cannabinoid levels by dry weight, making them extremely potent. Dabbing also delivers cannabinoids into the bloodstream almost instantly. One downside is the facility to overdose on the extract resulting in acute intoxication, which may result in passing out, nausea, or anxiety. Another is the risk of being burned by either the nail, blowtorch or superheated vapor.

(c) Vaporizing:

In 1994, BC Vaporizers coined the name "vaporizer", which is now used to refer to all vaporizer devices in today's market. Vaping is the process of heating dried bud or an extract using a device designed to boil (vaporize) cannabinoids at the optimal temperature for conversion of CBDA and THCA to CBD and THC respectively. Since the material is not being burned, the harshness and flavor of smoke is absent. As well, fewer toxins are being inhaled. Vaping gives the user a purer and richer tasting experience.

One must distinguish between vaporizers that are used for nicotine-based products and those designed for dried herb use. Glycerine or oil-based vaporizers sold by the tobacco industry have gained a lot of negative public attention since 2019. Many jurisdictions are wanting an outright ban on these devices.

Vaporizers typically sold by the cannabis industry pose less of a health risk as these devices are primarily designed for use with dried bud.

Vaping allows for a more rapid absorption of cannabinoids in the bloodstream. This is why many users report feeling the effects faster than smoking. It's also less of a bronchial irritant than smoking, which can result in a chronic cough developing.

Many vaporizers are compact, discreet and easy to operate in a public setting. This makes vaping an ideal choice for jurisdictions that still frown upon marijuana use.

From an investment point of view, both the manufacturers of these devices and those retailers selling an assortment of devices in addition to marijuana should do well as global demand heats up.

2. Edible Products:

Edible products containing cannabinoids are a discrete and easy-to-consume way of consuming cannabis. For those not comfortable with the idea of smoking or vaping cannabis, edibles are a good alternative. Cannabis can be added to many edible products and beverages. It can be used to make oils and tinctures or packaged in capsules for easy consumption. Here are the four most common categories of edibles.

(a) Tinctures:

Sublingual alcohol-based tinctures are made by dissolving a cannabis extract in high-proof ethyl alcohol. This alcohol-based tincture can be used by placing a drop under the tongue and allowing it to momentarily rest in the mouth to be absorbed sublingually.

The effects are typically felt within five minutes, with full effects being felt within twenty minutes. Although not as fast-acting as vaping or smoking, taken sublingually tinctures can be easily dosed.

For those who don't prefer the use or taste of alcohol, glycerin-based tinctures are an option. Glycerol is a clear, sweet-tasting viscous alcohol that gives wine some body. Ah wine that delicious nectar that helps white men dance.

A major advantage of any tincture is that the terpenes are more effectively delivered by mouth, since they are not being heated excessively and vaporized as in smoking.

It's the interplay between cannabinoids and terpenes that is important in the healing process. They also carry none of the harmful chemicals produced by burning and smoking cannabis.

Tinctures are discreet. Most bottles look like homeopathic medicine bottles. Stored in the fridge, they produce no telltale signs of cannabis odours.

Also, multiherbal tinctures are coming onto the market. Many herbs can be used with cannabis to create a synergistic effect. For example, passion flower, lemon balm and valerian root induce relaxation and sleep. When combined with a CBD-rich variety, you can induce a more profound state of relaxation.

(b) Cannabis Oil:

When an alcohol-based tincture is slowly heated to evaporate the alcohol, it produces a viscous oil that can also be used sublingually. Known in the industry as Rick Simpson oil, after the Canadian marijuana advocate, this concentrate is an easy way to determine an effective dose. By starting with a drop and increasing one's dosage gradually while monitoring the effects, one can arrive at an effective dose safely without any adverse effects.

(c) Beverages:

On a commercial scale, cannabinoid-rich tinctures can be added to a variety of alcoholic beverages, whether it be beer, wine, or spirits. One of the world's largest beverage conglomerates, Constellation Brands, entered into a partnership with Canopy Growth in 2019 to develop a new line of cannabis-infused alcoholic beverages. Do you think that there might be an investment opportunity there?

Along with the beer and wine industry, soft drink companies are also exploring ways of creating new lines of beverages. You'll soon see energy drinks, health beverages, coffee and tea drinks all being sold in various forms across many jurisdictions as the cannabis industry matures.

(d) Food Products:

Brownies, cookies, gummy bears oh my! The possibilities are endless when it comes to producing cannabis-infused food products. Ingesting cannabis appeals to many novice users as it doesn't require taking up smoking or drinking in order to benefit from the cannabinoids.

The effects of ingesting cannabis generally take thirty to forty-five minutes. This can pose a problem for novice users who'll have one brownie, not feel anything for half an hour and then munch on a second only to have the first brownie kick in. Too much could end up blowing your socks right off your feet. It's important to start with a low dose to determine how edibles are affecting you.

Also, be aware that the effects of ingesting cannabis are slightly different from inhaling it. Since the cannabis is passing through the digestive tract, a lower percentage of the active ingredients is made readily available by the body. However, the effects can stay longer in the body, which makes it a great choice for nighttime use. Effects typically last four to eight hours depending on the variety, dosage and your personal level of tolerance. This may be just the ticket to getting a restful sleep or going through the workday feeling better.

A disadvantage of eating your medicine is that if you're diabetic or overweight this approach may not be the best option for you when it comes to regular consumption, especially those delectable brownies.

Cannabis extracts can even be dissolved in coconut oil and formed into capsules known as canna-caps. These discreet pills can be taken virtually anywhere. Dosing becomes a lot easier with these handy little capsules. As with other edibles, the effects are usually felt within thirty minutes of ingestion.

3. Topical Products:

Topicals are cannabis extracts that are formulated to have a local effect by being absorbed directly through the skin. Most topical products are CBD-rich creams, ointments, oils and salves that are designed to provide relief for conditions such as arthritis, joint and muscle soreness, inflammation, and a myriad of skin conditions.

They typically contain very low doses of THC with most of the cannabinoids coming from CBD-rich plants. Traditionally, Cannabis Sativa (hemp) has been processed on an industrial scale to extract CBD for use in topical products.

Recently, certain CBD-rich varieties of Cannabis Indica plants grown on an industrial outdoor scale have gained increasing popularity in the production of topicals. This trend is sure to continue as breeders and cultivars develop varieties targeting specific applications.

Since the skin has both CB1 and CB2 receptors that topicals can act on for a therapeutic effect, they can do a good job of managing localized pain and inflammation. For those having to take opioids to cope with pain, cannabis topicals can drastically reduce the need to use narcotics or over-the-counter pain medications.

Topicals can vary greatly in how well they deliver cannabinoids and terpenes to an affected area of the body. Most topical applications have dissolved the cannabinoids into lotions and creams that contain glycerine, oil or alcohol. These carriers do a decent job of penetrating the outer layer of the skin.

Deeper penetration of the skin requires a carrier like DMSO (Dimethyl sulfoxide) to be added to the formulation. DMSO is an industrial solvent that's created as a by-product of paper making. Although DMSO is used world-wide for various health care applications, topicals made with this carrier require some precautionary steps. The main one is keeping any harsh or toxic substances away from the site of application as the carrier will transport these substances deeper into the body.

The best companies producing topicals are those that use the purest sources of natural ingredients. Consumers are demanding that businesses use fewer chemicals in their products. Avoid those that use preservatives like parabens or any artificial fragrances. If you're having a hard time pronouncing the chemical additive in a topical product, it might be a good idea to find one that has simple known ingredients like beeswax, aloe vera, eucalyptus, shea butter or Vitamin E.

The downside of using most commercially available topicals is that cannabinoids don't penetrate the skin very well. If you're suffering from deep tissue or joint pain, inhaling or ingesting cannabinoids often provides better relief.

Also, be wary of topical tinctures containing alcohol as they tend to create a burning sensation when applied to open wounds or cracked skin. This means that these products have a greater chance of falling out of favour with consumers. And if consumers aren't buying these products, then the businesses behind them may not be the best choices to invest in.

This goes for any marijuana product out in the marketplace. Knowing which products are in favour with consumers increases the likelihood of you finding businesses that would be good stock investment picks. With greater awareness as to what opportunities exist in the world of cannabis, the easier it becomes in finding appropriate stock investment plays.

～

3

WHAT AILMENTS DOES CANNABIS HELP?

Unfortunately, cannabis is not a cure for cancer or other major ailments. No peer-reviewed scientific proof has been presented to the medical community to date. However, cannabis does help one better manage and cope with various ailments.

Anyone looking for a one-step cure for what ails them is unfortunately adopting the wrong approach to health care. One's overall health is determined by a number of factors, such as physical fitness, mental health, nutrition and sleeping habits. The path to wellness is a multi-faceted approach.

It stands to reason that investing in businesses that take a holistic view of healthcare offers the investor greater chances of financially benefiting from a more diverse product and/or service line.

Later in this guide, we'll look at a number of specific stock investment plays to consider placing on your watchlist. Keep in mind that you want to place greater weight on those businesses that produce revenue from multiple income streams as opposed to just one or two.

If cannabis does help one cope better with illness, then for which common ailments does it have a positive effect? Both CBD and THC offer the user health benefits that have been documented anecdotally (through observations) and scientifically (through limited research).

Let's briefly explore 30 specific ailments with which cannabinoid-rich cannabis has been shown to help individuals better cope or treat what ails them. These insights should help you determine which businesses or industries are poised to see increased growth as demand for specific healthcare products ramps up.

1. Acne:

Acne is the most common skin disease across the globe. It's caused by the proliferation of sebocytes in the sebaceous glands that die, clogging the glands and inviting bacterial growth to occur. CBD has been shown to regulate this proliferation.

2. ALS Syndrome:

ALS is the progressive loss of muscle strength that often leads to death from respiratory failure and weight loss. CBD has been shown to be moderately effective in reducing certain symptoms, like pain, depression, drooling and appetite loss.

3. Alzheimer's Disease:

Alzheimer's is an irreversible brain disorder that involves loss of memory and cognitive abilities affecting one's ability to carry out the simplest daily tasks. THC has shown promise in helping with insomnia, pain, appetite loss, and anxiety issues. In general, cannabinoids play an important role in reducing inflammation, which is a major factor in how the disease progresses.

4. Anxiety Disorder:

Anxiety is the unpleasant sensation of apprehension when confronted with an unknown or fear-inducing situation. Cannabis has been used for thousands of years to treat anxiety. Next to pain, anxiety is one of the most frequent reasons why individuals take cannabis.

5. Arthritis:

Both rheumatoid and osteoarthritis can be treated with cannabinoids. Rheumatoid arthritis is an autoimmune disease that typically causes severe joint pain and damage, resulting in disability. Osteoarthritis affects the bones. It often causes cartilage loss in the spine, hips and knees.

6. Asthma:

Asthma is a common respiratory ailment. It's an inflammatory condition of the air passages whereby the individual experiences obstruction of the airway or bronchospasm. Recent research has shown that smoking or vaping CBD-rich varieties can be effective in treating inflammatory lung diseases and helps to regulate the inflammatory response in asthma.

7. Appetite Loss:

It is well-documented that THC-rich cannabis is known to give many users the munchies. Besides increasing one's eating motivation, THC also relieves pain, anxiety, and nausea, which are often associated with a loss of appetite. This makes cannabis a good choice for patients having appetite loss due to cancer, chronic disease, or HIV/AIDS.

8. Autism:

Autism is a complex neurobehavioral condition, often characterized by impaired communication and social interaction. Unfortunately, little has been published as to the merits of CBD as a potential treatment for autism spectrum symptoms. Recent studies in Israel that involve treating children with CBD have been showing promise. It may be that cannabidiol could be a better option in the future for helping to improve social interactions and calm repetitive behaviours, as opposed to our current potent medication approach.

9. Bipolar Disorder:

Bipolar is a mood disorder that has the individual experiencing recurring episodes of depression and mania, with depression being the most common symptom. Cannabis has shown to help relieve the anxiety often seen after a bout of depression or mania. It may also show promise in relieving other symptoms of bipolar disorder that are often treated with heavy pharmaceuticals prescribed by a psychiatrist.

10. Cancer:

Cancer is a condition where there is abnormal cell growth causing healthy tissue to be destroyed. Cannabis is not a cure for cancer. Cannabis should not replace current methods of treatment for cancer. Nor, should cannabis be used to help treat "all" forms of cancer. However, it can be used to help with the patient's overall condition, improving one's quality of life.

Cannabis has been shown to help address many negative symptoms associated with cancer, such as pain, insomnia, medical treatment nausea, weight loss and appetite. Varieties that contain a blend of THC and CBD often show better results than taking either cannabinoid on its own.

11. Depression:

Depression is a mood disorder accompanied by feelings of sadness, along with a loss of interest or motivation.

Severe forms of depression such as major depressive disorder (MDD) or depressed mood (DM) are best treated with current, conventional antidepressants. Where cannabis offers help is with mood elevation and anxiety relief. This is often seen when a patient has just been given a medical diagnosis or during treatment regimes.

12. Diabetes:

Diabetes is a disease in which insulin production by the pancreas is impaired resulting in elevated blood glucose levels leading to heart disease, blindness, kidney disease, stroke and other tissue damage.

Type 1 diabetes is typically seen with children and young adults who are unable to produce insulin. Whereas Type 2 diabetes, or onset diabetes, often occurs in adults suffering from obesity and poor eating choices. This is the most common form of diabetes.

Recent research is pointing to the use of the non-psychoactive cannabinoids CBD, CBDV and THCV for helping the pancreas regulate insulin levels. Research is still in its infancy when it comes to determining the effectiveness of certain cannabinoids in treating diabetes.

13. Drug Addiction:

Drug addiction to painkillers is a growing concern in the medical community, as is stimulant abuse.

CBD taken alongside opioid painkillers has shown promise in reducing the quantity of opioid medication required for pain relief. This translates into fewer opioids being prescribed and shorter treatment plans being set up, which ultimately reduces the risk of opioid addiction. CBD has also shown to reduce tobacco dependency in chronic users.

14. Fibromyalgia:

Fibromyalgia is a chronic disorder characterized by widespread musculoskeletal pain accompanied by fatigue, sleep, memory and mood issues. It is thought that fibromyalgia amplifies sensations of pain by affecting how your brain processes pain signals.

Cannabis has been shown to reduce stiffness, increase relaxation, improve sleep, and reduce pain in sufferers of fibromyalgia. Cannabis can be more effective in the treatment of fibromyalgia than current pharmaceutical options out in the market.

15. Gastrointestinal Disorders:

A myriad of gastro-intestinal disorders exist. Unfortunately, not all disorders benefit from the use of THC-rich cultivars. For example, appetite stimulation may best be achieved with low doses of THC as opposed to CBD. And THC varieties containing the terpene Caryophyllene help individuals better cope with diarrhea.

If constipation or inflammation along the GI tract are symptoms you're experiencing, then CBD-rich varieties can calm gut inflammation and increase motility. For gut pain, THC-rich varietals with high Myrcene levels may help.

16. Gerontology:

Cannabis products are being used to address many medical conditions that's face older patients as they age. Rather than take copious amounts of opioids to deal with chronic pain, cannabis has come into the mix as a safer alternative.

17. Glaucoma:

Glaucoma is an eye disease where the optic nerve is damaged by elevated ocular pressure. This often leads to loss of central vision and blindness. It is the most common type of irreversible blindness in the world. Both CBD and THC provide neuro-protective benefits.

18. HIV/AIDS:

HIV is a virus that attacks the body's natural defence against illness. AIDS refers to the set of symptoms and illnesses that occur in the final stages of HIV infection.

Severe pain caused by the HIV virus can be better managed when cannabis rich in THC and Caryophyllene is used. Insomnia is also improved when THC is administered as a sleep aid.

19. Huntington Disease:

Huntington disease is an inherited brain disorder where movement and thinking are impacted as the disease progresses. The disease causes uncontrollable jerking or writhing movements, difficulty focusing and recalling information, and a host of emotional illnesses like depression or obsessive behavior. It affects those in their 30's and 40's the most.

Cannabis helps to stabilize the disease but has yet to show any promise as an eventual cure. Cannabis can be used to treat many of the symptoms associated with Huntington disease.

20. Insomnia:

Insomnia is a psychological condition where an individual has trouble falling asleep or staying asleep at night. The most common treatment is sleep medication. However, inroads are being made into the dosage and delivery of cannabinoids as an effective and more natural alternative.

21. Migraines and Headaches:

A migraine is a severe, recurrent painful headache that often affects just one side of the head and can be accompanied by nausea, vomiting, or disturbed vision. Migraines can last several hours and even days. In contrast, common tension headaches are less severe and are often triggered by fatigue, stress, head injury, or medications.

Research has shown that the most severe form of headache, cluster headaches, can be treated with THC. In fact, many types of headache can be treated with cannabis.

22. Multiple Sclerosis:

MS is an autoimmune disease of the central nervous system causing problems with balance, muscle control, vision and numbness. Strong evidence supports the case that cannabinoids are neuroprotective, meaning that they can help decrease the severity of the disease by reducing inflammation and oxidative damage. The majority of people who have MS experience a relatively normal life span. The most common symptoms of MS that can be treated with cannabis are spasticity, insomnia, neuropathic pain and anxiety.

23. Nausea:

Nausea is an intense feeling of sickness with an inclination to vomit. Both acute and anticipatory nausea can be treated with cannabis. Acute nausea is often associated with a negative reaction to medications, especially opioids. Whereas anticipatory nausea is triggered by traumatic memories or fears.

24. Neuropathy:

Neuropathy is a disease or dysfunction of the peripheral nerves, characterized by pain or numbness in the back, face, hands, thighs or feet. Diabetes is the most common cause.

Chemotherapy-induced neuropathy seems to be more effectively treated with CBD or a CBD:THC variety than a THC cultivar alone. Whereas cancer-related pain seems to be more effectively controlled with THC alone.

Low to moderate doses of cannabinoids are typically prescribed for neuropathic pain.

25. Pain:

One of the most common conditions whereby cannabis is prescribed by health care professionals is pain. Pain comes in all shapes and sizes. It is well-known that THC can reduce pain symptoms.

The key to pain management is finding the lowest effective dose, as higher doses of cannabinoids may actually contribute to the onset of pain or in the case of THC, cause intoxication.

26. Pediatric Epilepsy:

Pediatric epilepsy occurs in young patients who experience recurring epileptic seizures. It's a neurological disorder that causes seizures or unusual behaviours and is often treated with pharmaceuticals.

Although THC use amongst children is strongly ill advised, CBD may prove to be an effective means of helping children cope with epileptic seizures better than conventional therapies and drugs.

High-CBD varieties have been shown to be effective in reducing the frequency and severity of seizures in many children.

27. Post-Traumatic Stress Disorder (PTSD):

Post-traumatic stress disorder develops in individuals who have been exposed to extreme traumatic stress that involves direct exposure to harm or death. It's often seen with returning war veterans. In the 60's, an estimated 50% of returning Vietnam veterans used cannabis to cope with this disorder and the stresses of war.

CBD has shown to be an effective treatment in reducing the memories that trigger the onset of the negative symptoms associated with post-traumatic stress. CBD could be another effective weapon along with cognitive behaviour therapy in treating PTSD.

28. Restless Leg Syndrome:

Restless leg syndrome is a nervous disorder that causes the incontrollable urge to move one's legs in order to alleviate any pain or discomfort. It can cause a sensation of creeping and crawling in the feet, calves and thighs.

Because CBD is a known to relieve anxiety, low to moderate doses have shown to provide some symptom relief.

29. Seizure Disorders:

A seizure occurs when abnormal electrical activity in the brain causes an involuntary change in body movement, sensation and behavior. Currently, anti-epilepsy drugs are the main treatment option for seizure disorders like Dravet Syndrome or Epilepsy.

What's exciting about CBD is that it provides a number of anticonvulsant effects with few adverse side reactions.

30. Stress:

Stress is the bodies way of reacting to a condition such as a threat, whether real or perceived, a physical challenge or an emotional strain. It manifests itself in the body as a massive release of hormones and chemicals such as adrenalin, cortisol and norepinephrine. Left unchecked it can lead to chronic anxiety or depression.

Next to pain relief, stress is listed amongst the top reasons why both medical and recreational cannabis users take cannabis.

Now that you have a better understanding as to how cannabis can be ingested in the body and what ailments benefit from cannabinoids, you'll hopefully be in the position to more readily identify investment opportunities.

And what do I mean by that, you may ask my little investment Jedi? In a nutshell, those companies positioned to deliver an assortment of consumer products that the marketplace wants are good choices for investment possibilities.

~

4

WHY YOU SHOULD BECOME A CASH FLOW INVESTOR?

Knowing how to invest in the stock market is only a small part of any solid wealth-building strategy. Before you should jump in with both feet, it would be helpful to first learn how successful wealth builders do it. Just because you've positioned some of your savings in the stock market doesn't mean that you're going to reach your personal financial goals any time soon. Investing blindly is about as useless as a screen door on a submarine.

So, how did that millionaire next door get to be so wealthy? The majority of self-made millionaires focus their time and energy on three types of smart investments, namely:

1. Their ongoing financial education in specific areas that will have a direct impact on their ability to grow their capital under all market conditions.
2. Their ability to acquire cash flowing assets, whether it be in the stock market, real estate or certain commodities.

3. Their ability to build systematized businesses that are able to generate passive income while they sleep.

Let's take a quick look at each of these smart investment vehicles and how they might help you down the road.

Vehicle #1: Become Financially Intelligent.

Kudos to you for having invested in your financial education by picking up this audiobook. The first step to wealth creation for anyone is learning how to generate passive streams of income that require a minimal amount of time to monitor. Along with these insights you'll want to determine how to preserve or protect your capital even under changing market conditions.

By learning more about various investment vehicles, you start to build a framework upon which you can start creating wealth for you and your loved ones. The most important tool that you can develop to ensure a bright financial future for yourself is your financial intelligence.

By systematically increasing your financial intelligence over time you'll empower yourself to solve the money problems that you may be faced with at this moment. And, yes, this is an ongoing endeavour.

When you improve the quality of the financial information that you use in your decision-making and differentiating between fact and opinion you set yourself up to be in a better position to tap into your financial genius.

This book is but one example of a helpful tool that will guide you in the right direction. I've listed a number of other resources at the end of your book to consider tapping into in the future.

Right now, making your financial education a priority in your overall wealth-creation strategy is the smartest move to make.

Vehicle #2: Acquire Assets.

After you've stopped monkeying around and gotten serious about improving your financial IQ, you're ready to start acquiring assets that put money into your pockets. In other words, you want to invest in those asset classes with a proven track record of generating cash flow from the investment.

Most people are familiar with stocks, rental property and commodities, which are the top three general asset classes that provide investment opportunities.

The focus of this book looks at the world of stock investing and shows you step-by-step how to implement an accelerated cash flow investment system that systematically puts money into your pocket. Your book also acts as a practical resource in outlining not only some of the top marijuana stock plays to consider, but how trends in the marketplace are going to affect your current decisions. Knowing how the industry is poised to evolve, gives you a significant advantage over most investors.

Whether you choose equities, real estate or commodities as your preferred asset class, please keep in mind that your focus should be on putting money into your pocket through positive cash flow.

Vehicle #3: Build Systematized Businesses.

This third smart investment vehicle is being mentioned to only give you a complete perspective of the three major areas where the resources of effective wealth builders can be allocated for creating sustainable wealth.

If you've got an entrepreneurial streak coursing through your veins, then building a low-start-up cost, systematized business that runs on its own even when you're not present is appealing. Should you be looking for an effective way to exit the rat race from a 9 to 5 job, then building a systematized business may be the answer. Many of us dream of the day when we're the masters of our own destiny and not having to succumb to an employer's chosen path for you. The cannabis industry provides many an entrepreneur with incredible business opportunities.

Please be aware that starting any business requires hard work and patience. Don't confuse "get rich quick", which is a distinct possibly for you, with "get rich easy". Unfortunately, there are too many self-promoting experts who'll tell you differently, especially those that are flaunting a particular product or service that you must buy in order to succeed.

A systematized business does have huge wealth creation potential that you could tap into should you have realistic expectations and develop an appropriate business attitude that factors in the amount of time and effort required to build your second or third stream of income.

In our household, we channel our hard-earned dollars into investments that either improve our level of financial education or purchase an appreciating cash flowing asset. By appropriately allocating our monetary resources towards building our dreams, it provides us with a greater sense of accomplishment, confidence, ongoing motivation and hope for a better future for the two of us.

I'm not going to tell you that investing in the stock market is your ticket to financial freedom. I don't personally know you. I don't know where you're at in terms of your financial education. Which means that I'm not going to pee on your leg and tell you it's raining. That would not only be uncomfortable but dishonest.

What I can help you with is in achieving a deeper understanding of how you could invest in the cannabis industry through the stock market. By the time you finish reading this guide, you should have enough background information to hopefully invest in the stock market with greater confidence.

Now that you have an idea as to where you can channel your future efforts, let's take a look at what you need in order to succeed as a cash flow investor. If you want immediate access to the profit stream that major corporations are benefitting from now and into the future, then the stock market is your answer.

Before we delve into seven mega-trends that could be profitable to you down the road, let's explore how you could optimize your stock market gains, while protecting your capital. What you're about to learn is going to change your whole perspective about stock investing. No longer will you fear the wide swings of the market that are a part of our normal economic cycle.

The stock market roller coaster.

The traditional approach to investing in the stock market is to place your hard-earned dollars in the hands of a trusted mutual fund advisor. Many well-intentioned investors who followed the advice of their mutual fund advisers lost a substantial portion of their hard-earned capital during the stock market crashes of 2001, 2008 and 2019.

Those passive investors who panicked and pulled their money out of the stock market into cash or bonds lost out. By cashing out at a loss they not only saw a loss of capital in their investment portfolios but when the markets started to quickly rebound, they missed yet another opportunity to get back to even. This collective ignorance has a long-term negative impact on one's ability to build wealth.

In 2011, a close colleague of mine expressed his frustration with his mutual fund advisor. His advisor had him switching from one fund to another over a 10-year period, chasing after returns. It was driving him up the wall.

His overall portfolio grew only by the additional deposits he had made over the years. He was bitter about what was unfolding and felt at a loss over what he could do.

What's even more aggravating are the lies that the financial services industry has been perpetrating over the decades about investing in the stock market.

Many mutual fund and financial advisers tout that stocks in the S&P 500 Index have generated an average return of around 10% over the past 90 years. This lulls investors into thinking that the stock market produces consistently high returns with little or no volatility. However, they don't tell you that markets do not climb upwards in a straight line.

The very nature of the stock market is that it is subject to wild swings, not unlike the waves of the ocean during a storm. Wouldn't it be fantastic if you could learn how to weather these storms? That would probably make you happier than a drunk fruit fly in a winery.

This deception about how the markets really function is often not taken into consideration in one's overall investment plan, especially in the short term. Without truly knowing how the markets function you are unable to incorporate money-making strategies that capitalize on the normal fluctuations of the stock market. This is what you'll learn how to do by the end of this book - on my boy scout's honor.

How do you build sustainable wealth over time?

To build sustainable wealth over time, you'll need to channel your efforts into two specific areas.

(1) Increasing your savings for investment purposes.

Everything hinges on the first pillar. If you do not make saving for investing a priority, you cannot invest. If you cannot invest, you cannot create the lifestyle that you desire. The first pillar to wealth creation remains your ability to move capital into investment opportunities as a result of your saving to invest regime.

Not only is saving an important habit to develop but you'll also need to determine where you'll invest your savings. Not all investment accounts are created equal. Some platforms are better than others in either deferring taxes or being tax exempt.

(2) Investing in market leaders.

This pillar is a structural part of your wealth creation machine. Buying shares of stock of those businesses that are the market leaders lends itself to a higher probability that the shares will appreciate in value more so than average stocks in that sector. The market likes businesses that have solid growth in earnings and cash flow.

We'll be looking for marijuana stocks that Mr. Market considers to be industry leaders. Although these players tend to command slightly higher stock prices, they do offer the savvy investor some assurance. The biggest advantage is that industry leaders that are in favour with Mr. Market, tend to appreciate more than the overall industry. They're also less vulnerable to wide market swings.

Why use an Accelerated Cash Flow Investment System?

Risk comes in all shapes and sizes. You risk losing purchasing power if your investment vehicle is unable to keep up with the rate of inflation, as is the case with most fixed-income investments.

You risk being able to generate higher returns because of fees that eat away at your potential capital growth as is the case with actively managed mutual funds. You also lose control over how you want to invest by turning over the reins to a fund manager.

You could conceivably risk having to wait decades in order to build up any appreciable wealth through index funds.

And, you must also resign yourself to amassing a fortune before being able to retire, since you've not learned how to generate additional income from your stock positions, if you invest solely in individual stocks.

Not many of us really can afford to fall asleep like Rip Van Winkle and wake up 20 years later realizing that the world has dramatically changed and that we've missed out on several lucrative investment opportunities.

Which brings us to using an accelerated cash flow investment approach.

The only risk that faces you now is in committing the time and undertaking the challenge of becoming a cash flow Investor. By taking up this challenge, your odds of becoming wealthy over time increase dramatically. The cash flow investment system that you're about to learn is based on two key factors that will accelerate your wealth building process even faster.

Time to explore both increasing the velocity of your money and reaching a point of critical mass.

~

5

HOW TO BUILD WEALTH QUICKLY

To build wealth quickly you need to increase the velocity of your money and reach a point of critical mass with your investments. These two concepts are fundamental to any wealth generation strategy. Unfortunately, they're not taught nor emphasized by the financial services industry, which would rather keep you hostage to being dependent on their formula for success.

The critical question that you need to be asking yourself is <u>when do you need to move</u> to another investment opportunity with more strength and momentum that allows you <u>to accelerate your wealth-building</u>? The first key wealth-building factor addresses this fundamental question.

Factor #1: Increasing the "velocity" of your money.

Charlie Munger, Warren Buffett's right-hand man, likens investing to swimming. Sometimes the tide is with you in a boom market.

Sometimes the tide is against you in a bear market. No matter. In both cases you still need to swim to make forward progress.

Talk to any successful investor and you'll quickly discover that they do not park their money and forget about it. They move their money from a good opportunity to a better one. It doesn't matter whether you're talking about stocks, real estate or other business opportunities. This strategy is known as the "increasing the velocity of your money."

With this in mind, your goal should be to acquire cash flowing assets and to continually seek out better opportunities that will get you closer to realizing your dreams.

The old buy and hold strategy that worked during the last major bull market of 2012 to 2020 is waning. Many financial analysts are predicting an average annualized growth rate in the stock market of between 4 to 7% over the next 5 years, not the 12%+ growth we've benefitted from over the past 7 years.

In order to accelerate your wealth building process, you have two plans of attack to consider.

The first is to look at how you can increase the velocity of your money within investments. This entails maximizing your profit-making potential by focusing on the combination stock appreciation in your core holdings and selling covered calls on those positions that offer that option. Each component adds to your overall return compounding over time to quickly reach a point of critical mass.

The second plan of attack for increasing the velocity of your money is between investments. This entails creating an investment mindset whereby you actively search out possible investment opportunities.

Develop the habit of looking for investments in which the odd one could present itself when it meets your specific buy criteria. It's at this point in time that you need to act quickly to move your money in order to take advantage of that window of opportunity.

By creating a winning mindset and planning your investments in advance you increase the chances of moving into these profitable opportunities.

Factor #2: Reaching critical mass.

Let me elaborate on the concept of reaching a point of critical mass with your investments. When you start out investing, the compounding effect of your investing slowly builds over time. At a certain point, the compounding effect of your cash flow that you're generating from your investments will exceed your annual household expenses and provide you with your desired lifestyle. It's at this point in time that you have reached a point of critical mass with your investing.

This number is different for each and every one of us. You must take into account all of your income sources, your current debt obligations and the lifestyle you want to create for yourself. Once you've reached this point of investing prowess, you can now look forward to being financially free and capable of maintaining your desired lifestyle through your investments.

My primary objective in this resource is to share with you the wealth of knowledge of the top investment educators currently engaged in the market today and do so through an accelerated cash flow investment system.

10 rules of wisdom from the investment guru's:

To help you formulate a list of investment rules designed to keep you out of trouble, let's take a look at what some of the top investment educators have to say about the subject. Every stock investor should have a pre-determined set of rules that they follow to guide them in their decision-making.

Your ultimate goal should be to create a system of rules that define specifically at what point you'll both exit and enter an opportunity based on likely outcomes or probabilities. Then, you'll need to stick to those rules when an investment triggers a course of action to take as the market moves either in one direction or another.

Here are the top 10 basic rules that many of the investment industry's respected experts suggest that you consider as part of your overall investment plan.

1. Own the market leaders; it's worth it. When the choice is among two or three companies in an industry, always go for the industry leader regardless of the price. Positive momentum favours market leaders. These companies tend to bounce back quicker when market corrections occur. And trust me they do occur frequently. You want to be on the positive side of these corrections.

2. If you want to build a sizeable position over time, buy in increments. Don't buy all at once. Always keep a small portion of your regular contributions in cash for those market breaks. You'll learn later in this book how to better time when to move into the market. Statistically, there are time periods that are more favourable for buying stock than others.

3. It's impossible to own more than 20 stocks unless you are a full-time stock junkie. The right-sized diversified portfolio where you can do it yourself is between 5 and 10 stocks. I like to mix up my personal holdings with the majority being individual stock plays, along with about 20% in ETF's. This helps to spread out the risk.

4. Sitting in cash on the sidelines may be a fine alternative. When the market is overvalued, take stock off, raise cash and get ready for the next decline. Sell strength and buy weakness in the stocks of companies you love and understand. What this means is that when everyone else is pushing up stock prices by buying as the market trends higher, you may be better off taking a contrarian approach, selling some stock to lock in profits. When the market self-corrects and overall stock market prices drop, consider moving cash back into the market buying those market leaders with the potential to reward you for your patience.

5. Buy stocks that you believe should go higher because of the fundamentals. Fundamentals are those financial metrics that describe how a business is doing from a financial perspective. You'll want to avoid stocks where the underlying business is bad or getting worse. Also, monitor those companies that have unfairly been beaten up despite solid fundamentals. They may provide great growth opportunities.

6. Take your profits off the table. Keep in mind that you don't have a profit until you sell. You should not confuse book gains with real gains. Those gains not taken can turn out to be losses down the road. Always take profits rather than worry about paying taxes and losing out on an opportunity entirely. Once you've reached your personal threshold as to when to cash in, monitor your holdings closely and sell your stock position once you see the stock starting to decline over a short period of time.

7. Take excessive emotional mood swings out of investing. Stick to your process of investing. Knowing that the stock market does not climb upwards in a straight line, means that you can more easily accept what Mr. Market is dishing out at the time. A patient, less panicked style of investing always generates a higher return. You can actually benefit more when there is volatility in the stock market. When you sell option contracts, the increased market volatility equates to receiving a higher premium. This happens so as to compensate option traders for the slightly higher risk.

8. Be flexible and open to change. Something good one month can turn bad. Stay on top of monitoring each of your positions. Industries come into and fall out of favour with investors on a regular basis. Some industries are cyclical in nature with stock prices reflecting this as money moves into and out of these industries. This is yet another reason why I favour short-term trades selling covered calls on stock that I own. My investment time commitment for my capital is one month with the possibility of rinsing and repeating the process if I have a winner.

9. Just because someone says it on TV doesn't make it so. We're seeing an incredible amount of "fake" news being generated in the media and on social platforms. It's becoming harder to assess whether what you're reading or hearing, is actually factual. Keep those "Spidey senses" tingling. Don't trust anything you hear coming from the rumour mill. You'll learn how to more effectively do your due diligence later in this guide. Once you learn what to look for as to what parameters make a company worth investing in, then and only then consider buying it. Base your decisions on the facts and not the personal opinions of others.

10. Cut your losses quickly. It's okay to take a loss when you already have one. If the entire market is trending upward and your stock position is heading for the dumpster, consider pulling the plug. You don't want to become a dumpster diver, do you?

With some careful investigation, you may find that what you initially thought was a potentially good investment has not panned out for you. A loss is a loss whether realized or unrealized. I rarely hold onto an individual stock position that's moving in the exact opposite of the markets for more than a few months. By controlling your losses, you can let your winners do the running. Recall, that we're trying to increase the velocity of your money moving out of poorer investments and into better ones.

Keep in mind that optimism or hope is not a good investment strategy. You need to plan in advance how you'll anticipate entering and exiting your positions so that you can optimize your returns. This may come as a foreign concept to you as most investors typically park their money.

I'm often asked why more individuals don't become successful cash flow investors. The biggest limiting factor to your success as an investor is not a lack of money to invest (although this may be a temporary challenge to overcome) nor is it the time it takes to become a do-it-yourself investor. It all boils down to focus. This means focusing initially on learning how to become a consistent, income earner in the markets.

The world will conspire to distract you - your phone, emails, constant text messages, social media - the list goes on and on. These distractors all have one thing in common. They pull you away from what you should be doing. That is, learning how to invest and find stocks that will create profitable streams of income.

A huge mistake is starting your day by checking your email and phone messages. If you check your email and messages first thing each morning, you're catering to someone else's agenda. You've lost control of YOUR agenda. Once you start responding to these messages, you've given up partial control of your day.

What's a better choice? You should start your day by focusing on your highest-value activities before you get caught up in other people's agendas for you. And what are your highest value activities? Those that improve your financial IQ and those that allow you to identify investment opportunities with a high probability of future success.

For me, my morning routine begins with learning more about the current and future changes occurring within the cannabis industry. I often ask myself:

How are current industry trends going to affect the major players in the market both short-term and a year or so from now?

More importantly, how can I best profit from these upcoming changes? For example, knowing that cannabis production will eventually become commoditized like wheat or corn production, I've invested in businesses that are positioning themselves in South America, which is projected to be a major supplier of cannabinoid-rich products as North American indoor production shifts to lower-cost outdoor facilities.

The biggest take-away from this chapter is that you should trade with rules if you want to trade with control.

The best stock investors look at each investment opportunity as a simple business transaction. When they feel that the opportunity has a high probability of success and they've comfortable with the way things are unfolding in the market they move into that position. They use a matter of fact, business-like approach devoid of negative emotions like fear, panic, anxiety or depression.

It's not that they're ignoring their emotions. It's just that they've learned to use a rational decision-making process rather than an emotional one. When you let the market come to you with opportunities, you no longer have to try so hard to make things happen.

Having a set of rules to play by, makes the whole process less stressful and more enjoyable.

$\sim$

6

THE F.A.S.T. APPROACH TO ACCELERATING YOUR WEALTH

An accelerated cash flow system is based on a combination of income and growth approaches generate higher returns than any one approach on its own.

The basic premise behind being able to accelerate your returns is that you'll build a portfolio of core growth positions. Ideally, we're looking for growing companies that are market leaders and best of breed in their respective market sector or industry.

A market leader has the general market and price momentum behind it. Many big institutional buyers look for stocks within a specific sector or industry that the overall market has fallen in love with. These stocks are in favour as evidenced by a positive growing trend in world demand for the products or services being offered.

For example, in 2011 and 2012 the mobile internet was one growing trend worldwide that had many technology stocks moving higher as a result of being in favour with the overall market players. Over the past few years both blockchain and artificial technology companies have benefitted from these trends.

The companies that are market leaders are those that are benefiting the most from the sale of their products and services in the worldwide market. They also tend to be the best of breed businesses within their industry. A best of breed business is one that has:

1. Solid fundamentals.

This shows up in the key financial ratios like the price-to-earning-to-growth ratio (PEG) or the price-to-sales ratio that are showing consistent double-digit growth rates and long-term debt levels that are under control. When looking at fundamental data focus on the rate of growth expressed as a percentage as opposed to comparing just the raw data numbers between companies.

Growth rates reflect how effective you are in increasing the velocity of your money. The raw data offers very little in the way of insights into how a business is doing financially.

2. A solid management team.

The person at the helm plays an important role in which direction the company is headed. You want to look for a CEO who comes across as having his/her shareholder's interest at heart and not his/her ego or the bonuses he/she might receive. Social media can be a great source of information as to getting a feel for those in positions of power within the business.

3. A competitive advantage.

Having a sustainable competitive advantage sets any business apart from other companies that are just along for the ride in a trending market. Determining if a company has a "significant" competitive advantage is easily verified by looking at the growth rates for earnings, sales, cash flow and book value.

Best of breed businesses have the staying power to be profitable over time, which in turn increases your profitability potential as an investor.

The F.A.S.T. Approach:

The acronym FAST will help you develop a step-by-step analytical approach to investing in stocks with the greatest potential to generate consistent profits. Once you've learned the basics, this simple template will save you time in quickly finding and assessing potential stocks.

As well, this template will optimize your ability to make money in the stock market by knowing which specific strategies to employ and how to safely move in and out of positions.

Each letter in the word FAST represents a specific series of action steps, namely:

Step #1: Finding potential growth stocks.

The letter "F" in the acronym stands for FINDING appropriate stocks that can be placed on a watch list and merit further analysis. You'll learn about 7 mega-trends and 3 cannabis industry evolutionary trends to keep an eye on. As well, I'll share 20 stock picks that merit further investigation as to potential plays. These insights alone will point you in the right direction for allocating capital in the stock market.

Step #2: Assessing the growth potential of each opportunity.

The letter "A" refers to ways of ASSESSING which stocks are market leaders. I'll show you step-by-step how to filter out those stocks that offer the greatest upside potential based on 9 popular indicators used by some of the top stock investors in the market. Granted these are not the only indicators for assessing business potential. The most important insight that I'll be sharing with you is to focus on those metrics that show a rate of growth.

Step #3: Strategizing the best way to create consistent cash flow.

The 3rd letter "S" looks at various STRATEGIES that both protect your investments and create capital appreciation. With the cannabis industry being so young, many investment opportunities are in growth stocks.

The momentum stock investing model you're about to be shown takes advantage of this growth characteristic while following the KISS principle. I don't want you running around like a headless chicken trying to figure out how to unwind a complex investment scenario. As they say: Keep It Simple Stewart.

Step #4: Timing your entry & exit out of positions.

The last letter "T" in the FAST acronym stands for TIMING. Despite what you may have heard contrary to not being able to time the market, I'll share a number of timing strategies that increase the probability of you coming out on top with your trades.

Would knowing when NOT to invest in the stock market and how to optimize your positions save you some frustration and money down the road? You bet it would Kemosabe!

Once you've had a chance to explore how the FAST approach to stock investing can accelerate your wealth creation in the stock market, you'll become a more confident and consistent investor.

◞

7
──────

FINDING WONDERFUL STOCKS

Time to get our hands dirty unearthing those cannabis-related stocks that might show promise down the road.

Before exploring a couple of dozen cannabis-related companies to place on your stock investment shortlist, let's look at a top-down approach to finding potentially great growth plays.

Using a top-down approach:

Every stock investor would love to own a portfolio of stocks that has the greatest potential for consistent capital appreciation over time with limited downside risk. The challenge is in knowing which stocks to place on your watch list of top candidates. Here's one stock selection strategy to help you with the decision-making process.

By looking initially at what the overall economy is doing, you can narrow down those cannabis-related businesses or industries that offer the best growth prospects over the next couple of years. Why just a few years? The harsh reality is that the economy expands and contracts on average every 4 to 6 years. So, trying to make realistic growth projections for time periods greater than 2-3 years becomes extremely challenging for any investor.

A short-term top-down approach takes a macro (or bird's eye) view of the economy. Imagine being a forester who focuses on looking at the health of the overall forest before checking out the individual trees that can be harvested.

Initially, place more emphasis on identifying market trends that will support certain sectors and then select those industries that will benefit from the trends. Once you have a feel for the overall market, you can drill down and select the best businesses in each industry or sector.

Here are three questions that help me get started in assessing the current market environment:

Question #1: Is the economy expanding, contracting or experiencing a recession?

This information is readily available from government sources, as well as from several major financial websites like Yahoo Finance, MSN Money or Morningstar. Look for official announcements indicating the state of affairs of the economy.

As you'll soon see, when the economy is growing or even experiencing sluggish growth, an accelerated cash flow investment approach works well. For most periods of time in the stock market, the probability of generating growth in your investment portfolio is quite high.

Question #2: What is the primary trend in the stock market?

By looking at a technical chart of a broad index such as the S&P 500 you can assess whether or not recent market conditions have been neutral (as in 2011), bullish (a positive outlook, as in 2012 to 2020) or bearish (a negative outlook).

When the economy is reeling from a pullback in the markets, this provides the smart investor with an opportunity to invest in market leaders at a discount. Both pullbacks and recessions are short-lived in comparison to the periods of growth in the stock market. It's reassuring knowing that markets generally trend upward over time.

Question #3: What is the interest rate trend?

If interest rates are rising, there may be competition from high-quality fixed-income instruments (like bonds) that may impact how money flows into and out of the stock market. More importantly, higher interest rates affect economic sectors differently.

Businesses listed on the major stock market exchanges can be loosely grouped into 11 economic sectors of like businesses representing key areas of the economy.

Examples of some specific observations that you can use to your advantage in screening for a promising economic sector of stocks are:

1. A low inflation rate trend will benefit the retailing industry and much of the cannabis industry.
2. A slowdown in consumer spending affects the consumer staples sector the least as these products tend to be purchased no matter what the economy is doing.

3. A strengthening economy benefits the consumer discretionary sector which in turn bolsters the recreational marijuana market.

4. A slowing economy is beneficial for health care and consumer staples, which are known as defensive stocks in a bad economy.

Seven megatrends to keep your eye on:

In keeping in line with our top-down approach, here are seven global trends that could provide you with some potential stock investing opportunities related to the cannabis industry.

Trend #1: Edibles.

Holy pretzel Batman! Not everyone wants to or is capable of smoking marijuana. This is where edible products fill the void. As bakers and candy makers develop their skills in creating pastries, cookies, bars, and candy treats, so does the potential for businesses to take off. Look for regional chains that may be taking their business to a national level as the demand for cannabis-based food products increases. In 2017 "Edibles" revenues amounted to $1 billion. By 2022, the edible market is expected to grow to $4.2 billion. Now, that could be a nice piece of the pie to indulge in.

Trend #2: Beverage Industry.

Constellation Brands has already made a substantial investment in the cannabis industry by partnering with Canopy Growth (CGC). Being one of the largest international alcoholic beverage conglomerates in the World, they have already positioned themselves to take advantage of the exponential growth in the industry.

Where cannabis consumption is already legal, winemakers and brew masters are already experimenting with cannabis-infused alcoholic beverages. Energy and soft drink producers are also looking at ways to incorporate cannabis into their products. Coca-Cola was in talks with Aurora Cannabis (ACB) to do just that.

While there are a few CBD beverages available today, with companies like Canopy Growth and Tilray researching THC beverages, these could be just the tip of the iceberg when it comes to possible cannabinoid drinks.

Trend #3: Pharmaceutical Industry.

The over 50 crowd is the fastest growing sector of the American population. As this segment of the population ages, they will require more services related to health care. Pharmaceutical companies and drug retailers should see steadily increasing demand for their products, even should a recession hit. The growth potential of the cannabis industry as more and more jurisdictions worldwide move to legalizing marijuana, will eventually filter into big pharma.

Market Analyst Michael Lavery says that big, traditional drug makers are already preparing for a U.S. market where cannabis is legal. He goes on to say that:

> "Pharma companies understand the potential for medical applications of cannabinoids and have products that could be ready to launch if/when U.S. federal law allowed it and if/when quality, consistent production was available at scale."

Pharmaceutical companies may not be able to patent natural molecules like CBD, but derivative molecules and unique production formulas are potential areas of proprietary technology.

Trend #4: Food Processing Industry.

Marijuana once harvested needs to be processed before it can be used for anything other than smoking and vaping. This is where the food and medical processing industries step in.

They provide the high-tech processing that enables the bud to be purified and converted into a form that the food and beverage industries use. In 2017 "concentrates" revenues were $1.9 billion and were 23% of the market. By 2022 it is estimated to be a $10.5 billion market while growing to a 36% market share.

In fact, in those states where the recreational use of cannabis is legal, fewer individuals are choosing to purchase buds for smoking and more of the general public is buying cannabis products made primarily from refined oils. Businesses that produce cannabis extracts will do extremely well in the future. And those that have an international presence will experience phenomenal growth over the next 5 to 10 years as global acceptance kicks in.

Trend #5: Pet Care.

The market for pet therapeutics is growing as more jurisdictions loosen their marijuana laws. If cannabis has health benefits for humans, could it also be beneficial in certain cases for our furry four-legged friends? You bet!

The American Veterinary Association has called for roadblocks on research be lifted. Over time we'll see more business opportunities evolve as a direct result of this growing trend. Cannabis pet care products could even surpass the traditional marijuana market in sales.

Trend #6: Bio Diesel from Hemp.

As technology advances so does the feasibility of bringing bio diesel products to market. Bio diesel made from plant-based material is a renewable energy source. Many nations are exploring ways to decrease their dependence on crude oil by leaning towards other alternative sources of power. Bio diesel made from hemp is one such alternative.

Once jurisdictions move to abolish outdated laws limiting the production of hemp, this'll open up the door for entrepreneurs to create new ways of generating energy. Taken to the next level, we could be seeing lucrative businesses producing bio diesel made from hemp on a national scale.

Trend #7: Building Materials from Hemp.

Two of the largest consumers of building materials are China and India whose economies will continue to grow over the next decade. Companies that should see a steady growth in sales as a result of increasing demand for construction material are those producing materials used in construction.

Unlike wood, which requires 40+ years between harvests, hemp can be grown annually. It also has physical properties that make it a better product than wood in some applications. This industry may be a few years away from being a major international player. However, once it does become established, you'll see some great stock investment opportunities unfold.

There you have it - seven trends in the cannabis industry that could provide you with some awesome investment opportunities down the road. But these are not all of the trends to watch for. Besides these particular industry trends, there are three industry evolution trends to keep an eye on over the next 5 years, namely:

1. Edibles Market Expansion:

Another factor to consider in your decision-making process should be what the financial analysts are forecasting for the cannabis industry. Cannabis businesses using a vertically integrated business model, whereby they cultivate, process and distribute marijuana products are poised to benefit the most from an expanding edibles market. So too will those specialty producers of consumables.

2. Federal Legalization:

Keep in mind that it is only a short matter of time before the U.S. Government legalizes marijuana on a national level. The growing trend is to see more and more State jurisdictions legalizing either medical and/or recreational use of marijuana.

Representative Jerrold Nadler and 2020 Democratic contender Senator Kamala Harris filed legislation in the summer of 2019 to federally legalize marijuana. If this or another legislation eventually passes, the Marijuana Opportunity Reinvestment and Expungement Act would remove marijuana and its psychoactive compound, THC, from the Controlled Substance Act.

In addition to this, the new federal legalization would also expunge previous criminal records and prevent agencies from using cannabis as a reason to reject benefits or employees. Furthermore, the legislation also proposes a 5% federal tax rate on all marijuana-based product sales. A portion of the taxes would be used for a new Opportunity Trust Fund to help people troubled during the prohibition era. Many other representatives and senators such as Cory Booker, Elizabeth Warren, Jeff Merkley and Ron Wyden have all co-sponsored the bill.

Once federally legal, major players will be able to move forward on expansion plans of providing a plethora of cannabis-related products through legal channels. Imagine getting in on the action when this development unfolds.

According to data compiled by Global Info Research, the global cannabis industry is expected to have a compound annual growth rate of 28% over the next five years. Exciting news for the little investor.

3. Cannabis Commoditization:

North American production of marijuana currently depends on a combination of climate-controlled indoor growing facilities and greenhouses to provide an uninterrupted supply of cannabis products year-round. Many grow operations struggle to keep production costs below $2/gram, especially those expansive indoor facilities in Canada and across the northern states.

Given that outdoor production of marijuana in South American countries can be 3 to 4 times cheaper, you'll see a shift in global production to more and more low-cost, outdoor operations. Cannabis is destined to become a low-cost production commodity. Knowing that this trend is eventually going to play itself out, wouldn't you want to be able to tap into these eventual changes in the marketplace?

Imagine seeing yourself investing in those companies that have growing facilities being developed in low-cost production environments.

Four great sources of insights:

Here are 4 tips that'll save you some time conducting your initial research in discovering those profitable best-of-breed businesses that can move you closer to reaching your point of financial freedom.

Tip #1: Check Out Free Websites.

Stock screening tools are available on several free websites such as Yahoo Finance and MSN Money. Using the search capabilities of each site you can find potential industries that might be of interest and then drill down to come up with a list of businesses that should have meaning to you.

Tip #2: National Business News Channels.

Look for potential stock picks on business news channels like CNBC, PBS or your favorite national business news station. Sometimes you can get great leads on businesses to consider in your initial investigation by watching financial news programs. Jot down the names of those potential companies that tweak your interest.

Tip #3: The Print Media.

The 3rd great source is through the print media. Books, magazines and newspapers are another source of potential companies to explore. Before buying any book or magazine or thinking about subscribing to any newspaper, save yourself some money by checking out the various sources at your local library.

There are a multitude of magazines to choose from, such as Forbes, Fortune, Smart Money and Smart Investor. As far as newspapers, check out the Wall Street Journal or The New York Times for ideas.

Tip #4: Stock Investment Websites.

What words of wisdom could you gleam from various stock investment blogs and websites? There's a lot of free information available on the web.

You can also check out paid subscription sites such as the Blue Collar Investor, American Association of Independent Investors, Motley Fool's Stock Advisor, The Street.com or Investor's Business Daily for suggestions.

Value Line has recently initiated coverage on several major cannabis companies. The company is a leading New York based provider of investment research. The Company's Value Line Investment Survey is now analyzing Tilray, Inc., Canopy Growth Corp., Aphria Inc. and Cronos Group. The fact that a major U.S. investment research company is now providing in-depth analysis and target-price projections bodes well for the industry.

As more analysts come on board and provide reports and ongoing research into the cannabis industry, more institutional investors will consider investing in this upcoming industry. With more institutional buyers comes greater stock valuations.

20 Best Marijuana-Related Stocks/ETFs:

What follows is a detailed list of some of the best marijuana stocks and cannabis-related businesses to consider placing on your watch list. Since mergers and acquisitions are commonplace within the industry, keep this in mind as you check out your potential candidates.

These stock picks are by no means an exhaustive list of potential plays to consider. I've identified 20 possibilities to place on your watch list. Once you've read through the following chapter that covers the various ways to assess the growth potential of each opportunity, you'll be more fully empowered to select those stocks that resonate with you the most.

As a side note, keep in mind that most cannabis and cannabis-related stocks are listed on Canadian exchanges that can be accessed through the Over-the-Counter market or Pink sheets. The "over-the-counter" market typically promotes small cap or penny stocks.

Since current U.S. Federal regulations limit U.S. based companies from raising capital or accessing federal banking services, most U.S. cannabis companies access capital through Canadian markets.

As well, when researching online for potential stock picks, look for those that also trade in the options market. These stocks typically have established themselves enough to be viable choices when you're looking to invest. You'll eventually want to be able to generate additional income and protect your initial investment through the use of covered calls.

Finally, potential investment considerations are listed in alphabetical order with those equities trading in the options market being presented first.

As previously mentioned, should you like to create an additional monthly income stream from your stock holdings, then consider picking up my book or audiobook "Covered Calls Beginner's Guide". This particular guide shows you how to generate an additional stream of relatively passive income with stocks that trade in the options market. The approach is a conservative one to employ.

Here are my top 10 Stocks Trading Options - listed alphabetically:

#1. Aphria Inc.

APHA: TSX

APHA: NYSE

Trading Range: $3 - 26/share

Market Capitalization: $5.5 billion

Aphria, produces and supplies medical cannabis in the form of cannabis capsules, oral solutions, concentrate syringes and tetrahydrocannabinol and cannabidiol vaporizers.

The company was founded by Leamington greenhouse operators Cole Cacciavillani and John Cervini on June 22, 2011 and is headquartered in Ontario, Canada.

In December 2017, Aphria announced that Shoppers Drug Mart, a Canadian pharmacy, would sell its production online.

Upon completion of the Aphria Diamond greenhouse, Aphria will be capable of producing 230,000 kg of cannabis annually with a focus on process automation. Having a low P/S ratio is a positive for the company.

Aphria also owns Broken Coast Cannabis Inc., licensed to produce 4,500 kg of cannabis annually. And the company has recently moved into the German medical cannabis market when its German subsidiary, Aphria Deutschland GmbH, received a domestic cultivation license issued from the German Federal Institute for Drugs and Medical Devices in April of 2019.

As part of its international expansion, the company acquired C.C. Pharma giving it access to 13,000 pharmacies across Europe.

Short-term, the company is currently focusing on expanding into the Canadian market. Since the stock is also being traded in the options market, it is presented here as being a good investment possibility when using a covered call option strategy for generating monthly income in the form of option premiums.

Aphria, Tilray and Sweetwater Brewing Company recently entered into a partnership to deliver cannabis beverages to the North American market.

Tilray and Aphria merged in the spring of 2021 thus creating a more competitive cannabis conglomerate.

#2. Aurora Cannabis Inc.

ACB: TSX

ACB: NYSE

Trading Range: $5 - 26/share

Market Capitalization: $1.5 billion

Aurora Cannabis, Inc. is a Canadian-based company that produces and distributes medical cannabis. It also produces and sells indoor cultivation systems and hemp related food products.

The company was founded in Edmonton, Canada by Terry Booth and Steve Dobler on December 21, 2006.

Aurora Cannabis is the 2nd-largest marijuana stock by market cap as of 2019 and is projected to lead all growers in peak annual output with at least 662,000 kilos, based on company estimates spanning its 14 grow farms. The company has an extensive and diverse production and distribution presence; more so than any other cannabis grower.

Despite nearly doubling its market cap since the beginning of 2018, Aurora's share price has actually declined a bit during 2019. The reasons are two-fold. The company has reported relatively steep operating costs in 2019. And recent acquisitions by Aurora in which the financing has been done primarily through stock transactions and not cash, have diluted its shareholders stake in the company.

Not surprisingly, Aurora Cannabis is one of the few large marijuana stocks not to have landed a brand-name partner or equity investment as of yet. Despite reports of discussions between Coca-Cola (NYSE:KO) and Aurora in September 2018, no deal ever materialized.

My personal take on this is that Aurora's consistent issuance of new stock, would have diluted Coca-Cola, or any equity investor, after their initial stake. This is the probable reason as to why we haven't yet seen a deal take place, and why Coca-Cola likely walked away.

In March 2019, Aurora did hire billionaire investor Nelson Peltz, the founder of Trian Fund Management, as a strategic advisor. Peltz has keen knowledge of the food and beverage industry; potentially being the perfect person to bridge the gap between the food and beverage industry and the cannabis industry.

No other marijuana company has as diverse a presence in foreign countries as Aurora. Between production, exports, distribution and research, its involved in 24 different countries. This should lead to a relatively diverse revenue stream over the long run.

Eventually, domestic Canadian production is expected to lead to dried-flower oversupply, whereby these overseas markets will come in handy as a means to offload excess cannabis. When this happens, it's possible that the more than 40 countries worldwide to have legalized medical cannabis could significantly buoy Aurora's sales. The moment the company becomes more reliant on high-margin global medical marijuana sales and less dependent on the domestic Canadian market is when Aurora Cannabis might be worth investing in.

In my opinion, this is one of the most aggressive and diversely positioned cannabis companies in the market.

#3. Canopy Growth Corporation.

WEED: TSX

CGC: NYSE

Trading Range: $13 - 57/share

Market Capitalization: $9.8 billion

Canopy Growth Corp., formerly Tweed Marijuana Inc., produces and sells medical cannabis. The company offers products including oils and concentrates, soft gel capsules, and hemp-based products. It focuses on the treatment of chronic pain, seizures, muscle spasms, nausea, and loss of appetite.

The company was founded by Bruce Linton and Chuck Rifici on August 5, 2009 and is headquartered in Smith Falls, Ontario, Canada.

As of June 2019, Canopy was the world's largest cannabis company, based on the value of all shares, or market capitalization. At that time, Constellation Brands Inc. controlled over 35% percent of the company. Constellation Brands is known for its extensive presence in the beer, wine and spirits industry.

Trading on the Toronto Stock Exchange as WEED, the company was the first federally regulated, licensed, and publicly traded cannabis producer in North America. It began trading as CGC on the New York Stock Exchange on May 24, 2018, as the first cannabis producer on the NYSE.

Tweed operates out of the former Hershey's chocolate factory in Smith Falls, Ontario, and operates the Tweed Farms greenhouse in Niagara-on-the-Lake.

In addition to operations in Canada, Canopy Growth has a partnership agreement in Spain with pharma company Alcaliber S.A. It also owns a subsidiary in Germany that imports medical cannabis, Spektrum Cannabis GmbH, and has a partnership with Spectrum Cannabis Denmark ApS, a medical cannabis grower.

The company has business ties in Jamaica, Chile, Brazil and Australia. In 2018, the company acquired Annabis Medical, a cannabis distributor in the Czech Republic and medical marijuana supplier Daddy Cann Lesotho in Africa. In February 2019 Canopy set up a partnership with the Beckley Foundation to distribute medical cannabis in the U.K.

In December 2018 the company acquired the German medical device company Storz & Bickel for $166 million. Storz & Bickel manufactures high-end, medically approved vaporizers like the Crafty and Volcano.

A tentative expansion step into the U.S. market was also made in April 2019. The company concluded a deal to pay $300-million for the right to buy cannabis company Acreage Holdings Inc. a company located in British Columbia but with a diverse portfolio of cannabis cultivation, processing and dispensing operations in the U.S. No actual purchase was made, but the agreement states that Canopy will buy 100% of Acreage shares for $3.4 billion if the American federal government legalizes cannabis.

I love Canopy Growth's strategic alliances that have it poised to enter the beverage industry and U.S. distribution markets as the North American industry opens up.

#4. Constellation Brands.

STZ: NYSE

Trading Range: $150 - 244/share

Market Capitalization: $46.3 billion

Constellation Brands, Inc. produces, markets, and distributes beer, wine, and spirits. It's the largest beer import company as measured by sales in the U.S. The Beer segment includes imported and craft beer brands like Corona, Modelo and Pacifico brands. The Wine and Spirits segment sells wine brands across all categories of table, sparkling and dessert wines with well-known brands like Robert Mondavi, Black Box, Paul Masson, Ravenswood Winery, Wild Horse Winery, Clos du Bois, Franciscan Estates, Kim Crawford, Meiomi, Mark West, Ruffino, and The Prisoner.

The company was founded by Marvin Sands in 1945. The company was incorporated as Canandaigua Wine Company, Inc. in 1972 and went public in 1973. In 2000, the company changed its name to Constellation Brands, Inc. to reflect the scope of the company and its range of brands. It is headquartered in Victor, NY.

In August 2018, Constellation brands acquired a 38% stake in Canopy Growth (WEED). The company plans on investing $4 billion for international expansion of cannabis-infused beverages and sleep aids.

Cannabis-laced beverages could be a $600 million market in the U.S. alone by year-end in 2020 according to a September 27, 2018 report.

The Quatreau beverage line will be sold across North America. The US operation includes 20 milligrams of hemp-based CBD.

Constellation became the first Fortune 500 company and the first major alcoholic beverage maker to take a minority stake in a marijuana business.

For the investor, Constellation Brands not only offers growth potential in the cannabis industry but also a consistent dividend paid out quarterly. This is yet another stream of income to tap into, not to mention being able to trade options on the stock.

#5. ETFMG Alternative Harvest ETF.

ETFMG: AMEX.

Trading Range: $10 - 35/share

Market Capitalization: $1.04 billion

This exchange-traded fund was founded in 2017. The ETFMG Alternative Harvest ETF seeks to provide investment results that, before fees and expenses, correspond generally to the total return performance of the Prime Alternative Harvest Index.

Here are the top 10 holdings of this particular ETF:

- GW Pharmaceuticals
- Aphria Inc.
- Tilray Inc.
- Grow Generation Corp.
- Canopy Growth Corp.
- Cronos Group Inc.
- Schweitzer-Mauduit International
- Altria Group
- Vector Group
- Hexo Corp.

The ETF pays out a dividend with an annual yield of 2.5% that's paid out quarterly.

This particular ETF also trades in the options market, which can generate some additional income in the form of premiums being paid.

#6. Cronos Group Inc.

CRON: NASDAQ

CRON: TSX

Trading Range: $7 - 15/share

Market Capitalization: $2.9 billion

Cronos Group, Inc. produces and sells cannabis primarily in Canada and Germany. Its portfolio includes Peace Naturals, Original BC (OGBC) and Whistler Medical Marijuana Company (WMMC).

The company was founded by Lorne Michael Gertner and Paul Rosen on August 21, 2012 and is headquartered in Toronto, Ontario, Canada.

Cronos Group Inc. is a diversified and vertically integrated cannabis company. The term vertically integrated refers to business models that look at marijuana sales from the cultivation and processing stages to marketing the product for medical and/or recreational use.

The company sells dried cannabis and cannabis oils under its medical cannabis brand Peace Naturals. It seeks to invest in companies either licensed or actively seeking a license, to produce medical marijuana pursuant to Canada's Marijuana for Medical Purposes Regulations. The company's other brands include Spinach and Cove.

Unfortunately, as of early 2021, Cronos remains extremely overvalued.

#7. GW Pharmaceuticals PLC- ADR.

GWPH: NASDAQ

Trading Range: $90 - 220/share

Market Capitalization: $6.8 billion

GW Pharmaceuticals PLC is a biopharmaceutical company, which engages in the discovery, development, and commercialization of novel therapeutics. It produces a lead cannabinoid product, EPIDIOLEX® oral solution CV, a pharmaceutical formulation of cannabidiol (CBD) that focuses on the treatment of seizures associated with tuberous sclerosis complex.

GW Pharmaceuticals and its U.S. subsidiary Greenwich Biosciences Inc. recently announced positive top-line results of a randomized, double-blind, placebo-controlled Phase 3 clinical trial of EPIDIOLEX® in the treatment of seizures associated with Tuberous Sclerosis Complex, a rare and severe form of childhood-onset epilepsy.

The company was founded by doctors Geoffrey William Guy and Brian Whittle in 1998 and is headquartered in Cambridge, the United Kingdom. That year they obtained a cultivation license from the United Kingdom Home Office and the MHRA, allowing the company to cultivate cannabis from seeds and clones to conduct scientific research concerning the medicinal uses of the plant.

The company also develops and markets Sativex, a cannabis extract drug, administered as an oromucosal spray for the treatment of spasticity due to multiple sclerosis. The company's presence can be primarily seen across Europe, the U.S. and Canada.

In 2011, GW Pharmaceuticals concluded a partnership with Bayer for the distribution of Sativex in the UK. Since 2012, the company has had an estimated annual production of 100 tons of medicinal cannabis.

In early 2021, Jazz Pharmaceuticals announced that it was acquiring GW for $220 per American Depository Share.

#8. Hexo Corp.

HEXO: NYSE

HEXO: TSX

Trading Range: $3 - 9/share

Market Capitalization: $1 billion

HEXO Corp. manufactures, produces, and distributes medicinal marijuana. It offers products through the Time of Day, H2, Decarb, and Elixir No. 1 brands.

The company was founded by Sébastien St. Louis and Adam Miron on August 13, 2013 and is headquartered in Gatineau, Quebec, Canada.

Incorporated in 2013 under the name The Hydropothecary Corporation, the company was created to meet the needs of the Canadian medical cannabis market. With the advent of the legalized market in 2018, the company became HEXO Corp, for both adult-use (recreational) and medical markets.

HEXO is a consumer-packaged goods cannabis company that creates and distributes innovative, easy-to-use and easy-to-understand products to serve the Canadian cannabis market. The adult-use market is served by the HEXO brand, while the medical cannabis market is served through its well-known Hydropothecary brand.

The Canadian Company is one of the largest licensed cannabis companies in Canada. It operates 1.8 million sq. ft of facilities in Ontario and Quebec and has a foothold in Greece for establishing a Eurozone processing, production and distribution centre.

HEXO has partnered with Molson Coors Canada to create Truss CBD which will produce cannabis-infused beverages for the Canadian legal market in 2020 and Colorado in 2021.

As well, with the passing of the recent U.S. Farm Bill to allow CBD extraction from hemp, HEXO Corp is well-positioned to seize a significant portion of market share in the U.S.

#9. Scott's Miracle Gro.

SMG: NYSE

Trading Range: $126 - 254/share

Market Capitalization: $13.5 billion

Scott's Miracle-Gro Co. manufactures, markets, and distributes systems and accessories for hydroponic gardening. The company was founded by Orlando McLean Scott in 1868 and is headquartered in Marysville, Ohio.

Scott's Miracle Gro's subsidiary Hawthorne Gardening provides hydroponic solutions (growing plants in a nutrient-rich water solvent, as opposed to soil), along with lighting, nutrient, and soil products, to U.S. cannabis growers in an effort to improve yield. In fiscal 2018, Hawthorne was responsible for $344.9 million in sales, or 13% of total corporate revenue.

The business made its first cannabis-related investment in April 2015, when it bought General Hydroponics, a 35-year old liquid nutrient maker, called by High Times Magazine as "the standard for hydroponic growers".

Scott's provides the savvy investor with a couple of options. First, even if the marijuana industry fell flat on its face and was hyped beyond belief, Scott's could always fall back on its core lawn and garden operations and remain healthfully profitable on a full-year basis. This makes it, arguably, one of the safest marijuana-related stocks to consider investing in. And second, with more and more U.S. states choosing to legalize marijuana in some capacity, the market for Hawthorne Gardening is growing.

In 2018 Hawthorne Gardening made an aggressive play, by acquiring Marysville, Ohio-based Sunlight Supply for $450 million, which included $425 million in cash and $25 million in stock. Sunlight Supply is primarily a provider of hydroponic solutions to the cannabis industry.

For the conservative investor looking for exposure in the cannabis industry, this particular company may check off a number of desirable boxes that of exposure to several industries, options plays and long-term growth potential.

#10. Tilray Inc.

TLRY: NASDAQ

Trading Range: $4 - 67/share

Market Capitalization: $3 billion

Tilray is a global pioneer in the research, cultivation, production and distribution of cannabis and cannabinoids. Its dried cannabis products and cannabis extracts currently serve tens of thousands of patients and consumers in 12 countries spanning 5 continents.

The company was founded on January 24, 2018 and is headquartered in Nanaimo, British Columbia, Canada.

Tilray has operations in Australia, New Zealand, Germany, Portugal and Latin America.

In July 2018 the company became the first cannabis company to IPO on the NASDAQ and trades under the ticket symbol TLRY.

In September 2018, Tilray became the first Canadian cannabis company to legally export medical cannabis to the U.S. for a clinical trial.

In December 2018, the company signed a deal with Novartis AG's subsidiary Sandoz generic pharmaceuticals to sell, distribute and co-brand Tilray's non-smokable/non-combustible medical cannabis products in legal markets worldwide.

In October 2018, Tilray launched High Park Company, which operates in the adult recreational cannabis market to establish unique adult-use brands in Canada.

Also, in 2018, Tilray announced a $100-million joint venture with the world's largest brewer, AbInBev to research non-alcohol THC and CBD-infused beverages, through their respective subsidiaries Labatt Breweries and High Park Company.

In 2019, Tilray signed a creative $250-million revenue-sharing deal with U.S. based brand company Authentic Brands Group. The partnership will see Tilray leveraging some of ABG's biggest brand names like, Juicy Couture, Greg Norman and Nine West to create cannabis products, powered exclusively by Tilray. ABG has a portfolio of over 50 brands.

Also, in 2019, Tilray acquired Manitoba Harvest, a hemp and natural foods producer in Winnipeg, Manitoba, for up to $310 million. The deal is subject to certain revenue milestones being met. Manitoba Harvest distributes its products to over 16,000 retail locations in the United States and Canada.

Tilray plans on expanding its manufacturing footprint from 1.1 million to 1.3 million square feet worldwide over the next year.

Although its international sales lag behind Canopy Growth, its production facility in Portugal should accelerate the company's international initiatives.

This was one of my favorite stock picks in 2019. Although the company may lag behind those competitors aggressively going after the cultivation market, Tilray is hedging its bet that eventually marijuana will become commoditized and that by focusing on other aspects of cannabis production and product development, it may just prove to be more fruitful down the road.

Here are my top 10 Stocks that Do Not Trade Options:

Some of these companies have the potential to be big-time winners in the cannabis industry as both domestic and international markets open up even more.

Look for opportunities that'll play into either the business trends that the cannabis industry should experience over the next five years or the industry evolution trends that'll see dramatic changes in the edibles and beverages market, federal legalization and eventual commoditization of plant production.

#11. Acreage Holdings.

ACRG.U: CNSX

ACRGF: OTC

Trading Range: $2 - 9/share

Market Capitalization: $790 million

Acreage Holdings, formerly known as High Street Capital Partners, is a vertically integrated, multi-state operator in the cannabis industry whose business operations include cultivating, processing, distributing and retailing cannabis. The company earns most of its revenue from its retail dispensaries located in New England, the Mid-Atlantic, and the Mid-west.

The company is domiciled in British Columbia, Canada.

In late 2018, Acreage Holdings acquired Michigan-based Blue Tire Holdings LLC. The 55,000-square-foot facility in Flint, Michigan will grow high-end cannabis indoors and serve as the company's flagship retail location. Acreage has cultivation, processing and dispensing licenses or agreements with holders in 19 states. It also manages a chain of retail stores called The Botanist.

In April 2019, Canopy Growth (CGC) agreed to pay $300 million cash for the right to acquire Acreage for $3.4 billion worth of stock. This deal is conditional in the event that cannabis becomes permissible under federal law in the United States. Many financial analysts for the cannabis industry feel that this deal is less than desirable for Acreage shareholders.

In the spring of 2021, Acreage Holdings and Medterra CBD launched a joint collaboration project making them one of the largest CBD innovators in North America.

#12. Cresco Labs.

CL: CNSX

CRLBF: OTCQX

Trading Range: $3 - 17/share

Market Capitalization: $5 billion

Cresco Labs Inc. engages in the business of cultivating medical grade cannabis, manufacturing medical products derived from cannabis cultivation, and distributing such products to medical or adult use consumers. It focuses on regulatory compliance while working to develop condition-specific strains of cannabis and non-invasive delivery methods.

The company was founded by Charles Bachtel, Joseph Caltabiano, Dominic Sergi, Rob Sampson, and Brian McCormack on July 6,

1990 and is headquartered in Chicago, Illinois. All the revenues of the company are generated in the United States.

Cresco Labs focuses on entering highly regulated markets with outsized demand potential and strong regulatory structures. Its impressive speed-to-market gives Cresco a distinct competitive advantage as it replicates its model to expand its national footprint.

Cresco's products are tailored to all major consumer segments such as everyday cannabis users, medicinally focused markets and connoisseur grade consumers. They even produce chef-inspired edibles by James Beard award-winning pastry chef Mindy Segal.

The company distributes its products to dispensaries nationwide, including several operated by its team. It has ownership interests in Illinois, Pennsylvania, Ohio, California, Maryland and Arizona. Its product lines include, Remedi, Mindy's and Reserve.

Cresco Labs Inc. is one of the largest vertically integrated multistate cannabis operators in the United States and has recently acquired CannaRoyalty Corp.'s Origin House (OH) that will provide greater access to various cannabis markets.

#13. Curaleaf Holdings Inc.

CURA: CNSX

CURLF: PNK/OTC

Trading Range: $6 - 23/share

Market Capitalization: $12.7 billion

Curaleaf is an integrated medical and wellness cannabis operator in the United States. It operates primarily on the East Coast with major acquisitions in Arizona, Florida, Maryland and New York.

In 2019, Curaleaf announced the acquisition of Select, the leading cannabis wholesale brand. The Select transaction would combine Curaleaf's retail locations, vertical integration, wellness brand and strong East Coast market presence with Select's wholesale model, lifestyle brand and leading West Coast market presence.

The combination of Curaleaf and Select will bring together the largest retailer and largest wholesaler, with the leading wellness and lifestyle brands in the United States, providing substantial opportunities to accelerate revenue growth, achieve significant cost savings and expand overall margins.

Curaleaf acquireed GR Companies Inc., which is also known as Grassroots, in a deal valued at $875 million in cash and stock in July 2020. This increased Curaleaf's presence from 12 to 19 states, making it the world's largest cannabis company by revenue. The combined company will have 131 dispensary licences, 68 operational locations, 20 cultivation sites and 26 processing facilities.

Like many large cannabis companies, Curaleaf supports clinical trials that advance research into the many ways medical marijuana can be used.

The company is led by an experienced management team with backgrounds in health care, retail, non-profit and financial services.

Curaleaf's mission is to develop safe, effective, and innovative marijuana products. They intend on becoming the leading vertically integrated, multi-state cannabis operator in the United States.

#14. Green Thumb Industries Inc.

BYU: TSX-Venture

GTBIF: PNK/OTC

Trading Range: $5 - 40/share

Market Capitalization: $6.5 billion

Green Thumb Industries is a vertically integrated cannabis operator that focuses on limited-licenced markets in the United States. Like many vertically integrated cannabis businesses, it manufactures and distributes branded cannabis products.

The company was founded by Benjamin Kovler on February 18, 2002 and is headquartered in Chicago, Illinois.

Green Thumb Industries manufactures, distributes, and sells various cannabis products for medical and adult-use in the United States. It offers cannabis flower, concentrates, edibles, topicals and other cannabis products under the Rhythm, Dogwalkers, The Feel Collection, and Beboe brands.

The company distributes its products primarily to third-party retail stores, as well as selling finished products directly to consumers in its own Rise retail stores. As of May 2, 2019, it owned and operated 18 retail stores, as well as had licenses for 77 locations across 12 U.S. markets.

Green Thumb Industries generated operating revenues in five markets in 2019: Nevada, Illinois, Pennsylvania, Massachusetts and

Maryland. It has deals in place to enter Florida, Ohio, New Jersey, Connecticut, California and Colorado. The company will go from 14 open stores as of 2018 to an additional 15 to 20 stores being added in 2019.

Green Thumb Industries has substantial expansion plans that are generally being overlooked with the stock being mostly flat from 2017 to 2020. Their revenue totals are some of the largest in the healthcare sector for cannabis stocks even including the Canadian licenced producers that grab all of the headlines. Expect U.S. cannabis stocks to surge with federal relaxation of cannabis laws making them some of the best investments in the long run.

#15. Harvest Health & Recreation.

HARV: CSE

HRVSF: OTCQX

Trading Range: $1 - 4/share

Market Capitalization: $1 billion

Harvest Health & Recreation is a vertically integrated cannabis company with one of the largest and deepest footprints in the U.S.

The Company specializes in operating cultivation, dispensary, and production facilities.

Headquartered in Tempe, Arizona, Harvest Health & Recreation is a multi-state cannabis operator. It has primarily expanded throughout Arizona, Maryland, and Pennsylvania.

Subject to completion of its announced acquisitions, Harvest will have the largest footprint in the U.S., with rights to 230 facilities, of which 142 are retail locations across 17 states.

Since 2011, the company has been committed to aggressively expanding its Harvest House of Cannabis retail and wholesale presence throughout the U.S. It continues to acquire, create and grow leading brands for patients and consumers nationally.

One merger that's particularly promising for Harvest is its combination with the Chicago firm Verano, given that the Illinois legislature voted to legalize recreational marijuana in June of 2019. Verano is expected to add licenses throughout the Midwest and East Coast, add edibles to Harvest House's brand suite and further strengthen overall operations.

Harvest's ability to combine size, scale, capital, regulatory expertise and operational excellence have been paramount to its success.

#16. Horizons Marijuana Life Sciences ETF.

HMMJ.U: TSX

Trading Range: $8 - 16/share

Market Capitalization: $500 million

Horizons HMMJ seeks to replicate, to the extent possible, the performance of the North American Medical Marijuana Index, net of expenses. The North American Medical Marijuana Index is designed to provide exposure to the performance of a basket of North American publicly listed companies with significant business activities in the marijuana industry.

The top 10 Holdings are:

- Aphria Inc.
- Canopy Growth Corp.
- Cronos Group Inc.
- Innovative Industrial Properties Inc.
- Tilray Inc.
- Scott's Miracle-Gro Co.
- GW Pharmaceuticals PLC
- Grow Generation Corp.
- Village Farms International Inc.
- Charlotte's Web Holdings Ltd.

This ETF pays out an annual dividend of 3 % on a quarterly basis.

Industry-related ETFs are a popular way of investing in the cannabis industry given that you're holding a basket of stocks and that the management fees for these funds are low as compared to your average mutual fund.

#17. MariMed Inc.

MRMD: PNK/OTC

Trading Range: $0.13 - $1.00/share

Market Capitalization: $258 million

MariMed is one of the largest multi-state cannabis operators in the U.S. The company develops precision-dosed cannabis-infused products designed for specific medical conditions and related symptoms. Its products are licensed under the brands of Kalm Fusion, Betty's Eddies, and Nature's Heritage, in the form of dissolvable strips, tablets, powders, microwaveable popcorn, and fruit chews.

The company was founded by Robert Fireman and Jon Levine on January 25, 2011 and is headquartered in Norwood, Maine.

MariMed currently distributes its branded hemp and CBD products in select states and is expanding licensing and distribution to numerous additional markets encompassing thousands of dispensaries, pharmacies and wholesalers.

They hold 13 cannabis licenses for cultivation, production and dispensaries across six U.S. states. MariMed is currently managing over 300,000 square-feet of premier cannabis facilities.

MariMed has made a strategic partnership with GenCanna, a Kentucky-based, vertically integrated hemp producer of GMP-compliant CBD oils and isolates. It has focused its attention on expanding its presence in the hemp-derived CBD market with premium materials and products.

They also intend to extend their geographic reach through direct ownership of cannabis licenses and related seed-to-sale operations in the U.S. and internationally.

#18. MedMen Enterprises Inc.

MMNFF: PNK/OTC

MMEN: CNSX

Trading Range: $0.10 - $1.47/share

Market Capitalization: $304 million

MedMen is another one of the largest retail cannabis companies in the U.S. with multiple assets and operations in California, Nevada, and New York. The company owns and operates licensed cannabis facilities in cultivation, manufacturing and retail.

MedMen was founded in 1987. The company went public in May 2018 on the CSE (Canadian Stock Exchange).

The company's primary objective is to build the MedMen brand through flagship retail stores. In 2021, they had 29 operational retail locations with an additional 36 retailers to come online nationwide that'll be located in 12 states.

They are first and foremost a cannabis retailer. Their focus is on strengthening their retail brand and growing their retail footprint in key markets.

#19. OrganiGram Holdings Inc.

OGRIF: PNK/OTC

OGI.WT.A: TSX-V

Trading Range: $1 - 7/share

Market Capitalization: $753 million

OrganiGram is a leading licenced producer of cannabis in the Canadian market. The company's Moncton campus production facility is projected to be able to produce dried flower or equivalent cannabis of approximately 113,000 kg per year and will also house state of the art added-value manufacturing equipment that'll produce world-class infused chocolate products.

OrganiGram is based in Moncton, New Brunswick and has two buildings on 14 acres with 480,000 square feet of production space at full build out.

The company has developed a portfolio of legal adult use recreational cannabis brands including The Edison Cannabis Company, Ankr Organics, Trailer Park Buds and Trailblazer.

OrganiGram has been selected as one of the four Canadian launch partners of PAX Era, the premium oil vaporizer created by PAX Labs, Inc. PAX is a leading consumer technology brand in the design and development of premium vaporizers for dry flower and concentrates.

#20. Charlotte's Web Holdings, Inc.

CWBHF: PNK/OTC

Trading Range: $2 - 8/share

Market Capitalization: $677 million

This top CBD production company is an up-and-coming player in the cannabis industry. They have very good brand recognition in the U.S. with the creation of the Charlotte's Web CBD cannabis strain that helped Charlotte Figi with her Dravet Syndrome.

Charlotte's Web Holdings produces and distributes hemp-based, cannabinoid wellness products. They produce a variety of tinctures, capsules, topical products, powdered supplements, single-use beverages, and sport/professional products.

The company was founded by Joel and Jared Stanley in 2013 and is headquartered in Boulder, CO.

Charlotte's Web distributes its products through e-commerce, select wholesalers and a variety of brick-and-mortar retailers, such as Kroger, which is slated to carry CBD topical products in 1350 store locations across 22 states.

Narrowing Down the Possibilities:

Now that you have a better idea as to how to find potential candidates, let's narrow down your watch list by looking at assessing the growth potential of each prospect. To do so, I'll share some basic selection criteria to help you assess the viability of your picks.

The identification and assessment of potential stocks can be a tedious process. Wherever possible, the smart cash flow investor will use those free or inexpensive tools that make the selection process faster and easier.

The extent of research and effort that you'll put in boils down to three factors:

1. How much time you have to realistically do your due diligence.
2. Whether or not your stock will be held long-term as an investment, or short-term as a cash flow trade as in the case of a monthly covered call.
3. Your personal preference as to how much money you could allocate to tap into the speed and convenience offered by subscription sites.

My advice to every upcoming investor is to initially learn how to use the assessment criteria as part of your overall selection process. Once you understand how each particular factor helps you identify those cannabis industry leaders offering the greatest upside potential, then you can begin to streamline your selection process as you become more familiar with what each factor has to offer.

I can also offer these words of wisdom that may help guide you in your decision-making process:

1. The longer your holding period for your stock pick the more effort you should put into the assessment process. For example, if you are looking for a quality dividend-paying stock or ETF that you would like to hang onto for at least one year, then take the time to check out the business or holding thoroughly.
2. The greater the reward and risk involved in the selection of a particular investment strategy the more time you should spend assessing the upside potential of the stock you're considering.

When narrowing down your watchlist, ask: What is the business's path to profitability? Then, look for cannabis and cannabis-related stocks that address how they are:

- lowering their production costs.
- diversifying their business interests.
- going about getting exposure in the international market.
- building brand strength and recognition.
- ensuring product quality and compliance.

As to what to expect over the next couple of years. What we saw in 2019 was that most cannabis investors were chasing headlines, pumping money into specific stocks with the release of the latest news in the industry. This created a high level of volatility in the options market for cannabis stocks, which can translate into good news for the knowledgeable options trader who can benefit from richer premiums being paid out.

You may be asking yourself if this is yet another bubble to burst like the cryptocurrency bubble. Although the industry will experience some wild swings over 2021, what's different about cannabis is that there is an underlying product that is growing in demand.

Expect 2021 to be a year of mergers, acquisitions and joint ventures as the industry goes through its current fragmentation phase. During the next couple of years, taking a basket approach to investing in marijuana-related stocks can reduce some risk. Look for companies that either produce marijuana products or those that support the industry with technology or services.

Let's take a look at some of the personal favorite assessment criteria used by many successful stock investors and educators in today's marketplace.

~

8
ASSESSING GROWTH POTENTIAL

Now that you have a shortlist of potential investment candidates, it's time to assess the profitability of each selection. Ideally, we want to be able to use company financials dating back at least 5 years in our analysis process. A 5-year time span provides enough financial data to calculate some key growth rate metrics.

In reality, many cannabis investment candidates don't have a long, proven track record of generating growing revenue streams. The industry is still too young and having to constantly adjust to major industry developments. This increases stock volatility within the industry, which can be frustrating for a "buy - hold - pray" investor and a blessing for an option's trader.

Three key Assessment Steps:

Whether you're looking for a specific cannabis stock or one in a related industry, there are three key steps to follow when picking potential stocks for your investment portfolio. Your primary objective is to analyze several businesses and determine which ones have the greatest upside potential for growth.

In essence, before you commit any of your hard-earned cash to any stock purchase, you'll be doing an in-depth "best-of-breed" analysis of several businesses. This analysis follows these three steps:

Step #1: Compare the fundamentals of the business over preferably a 5-year period of time. Fundamentals refer to the rate of growth of sales, income, and equity in comparison to the on-going expenses and liabilities. Ideally, you're looking for businesses with a long track record of consistently growing shareholder equity year to year. You'll soon learn about nine criteria to consider using for assessing industry leaders.

Step #2: Determine the type and extent of the competitive advantage or economic moat that the business has created that sets it apart from its competition. We'll explore seven types of economic moats in a moment.

Step #3: Assess the management's focus and compensation. You're looking for CEO's that are passionate about their work and the importance they place on creating real long-term sustainable value for their shareholders. Look for management teams that are fairly compensated for their efforts as opposed to the few who rip off unsuspecting shareholders with outrageous bonuses or ridiculous parachute clauses when they are forced to leave.

Step 1 - Screen potential stocks using these top 9 assessment criteria:

Ideally, we want to be able to quickly identify fundamentally sound businesses with upside growth potential using just a handful of assessment criteria. I don't know about you, but I prefer having to keep track of fewer variables in my decision-making process than having too much information at my disposal.

Let me jump right in with a list of the top 9 indicators that I like to use for both finding great stocks and assessing their potential. This list is by no means an exhaustive or exclusive list. It has served me and other cash flow investors well in identifying market leaders who are top-notch businesses. I've based my list on what several of the top investment experts have used in their selection process.

By looking at recent best practices in the stock investment industry, I was able to drill down and create a short list of the most popular criteria for finding wonderful businesses for your stock portfolio.

Let's not dilly dally. Here are the top 9 indicators that many of the top dogs like to use for finding great stocks:

1. Return on invested capital (ROIC) being greater than 10%.
2. Book value per share growth rate (BVPS) of at least 10%.
3. Earnings per share growth rate (EPS) being greater than 10%.
4. Revenue or sales growth rate greater than 10%.
5. Cash flow growth rate of 10%.

6. Debt-to-equity ratio (D/E) which should be low and preferably less than 0.5.

7. Price-to-earning-to-growth ratio (PEG) of less than 1.0.

8. Price-to-sales ratio (P/S) which should be low, preferably under 1.0.

9. Relative strength index (RSI) should be high for momentum plays within a range of 60 to 80. This is a technical chart indicator.

All of the "growth rates" listed above should ideally be consistent over a 5-year period. In general, what I look for is consistent growth in earnings over a period of 5 to 7 years and with the capital being generated being put to good use by the management to grow the business.

Now, don't get into a tizzy. I realize that many cannabis companies don't have a 5-year track record for sales and revenue growth. Many of these players just recently listed themselves on the stock market. This makes it a bit more challenging trying to figure out whether a company will be profitable moving forward. To quote the great Elmer Fudd we'll need to: "Be vewy, vewy careful."

Alternatively, you may wish to investigate those companies that are looking at partnering with some of these up-coming cannabis companies. Investing in well-established companies willing to partner with cannabis companies may be the ticket, as new markets open up. Try to choose stocks in well-established industries like the food and beverage industry for potential picks.

If you can't invest directly in a cannabis company at least you can be a part of a growing industry by aligning yourself with those companies that have an underlying agreement to do future business together. Refer back to the notes covering the 25 potential stock picks for companies looking at partnering with these cannabis leaders.

Now that you have an idea as to which factors you can use in your assessment process let's take a look at how each of these 9 factors can be used in our assessment process.

Five key growth rates:

A common question that I am asked is: Which financial numbers do I need to listen to in order to confirm the strength of a business?

Ideally, you want to be able to use just a handful of indicators that help you determine whether you can both trust and predict that the business can deliver double-digit returns in the future. We want to keep the process as simple as possible. We also want to be able to compare rates of change as opposed to the raw numbers. Monitoring rates of change goes hand-in-hand with the concept of increasing the velocity of your money. Some of the most popular indicators and the top five that I personally use in my assessment process are:

Factor #1: Return on Investment Capital (ROIC).

The ROIC is the rate of return a business makes on the cash it invests every year. The ROIC is a measure of how effective a company uses its own and borrowed money invested in its operations. I place greater weight on this fundamental ratio as it tells the investor how effective the business is in using invested capital. This ratio is a strong predictor that the business has a competitive advantage in its industry.

Although important, do not place too much weight on this metric should the stock be relatively new to the market. Expect to see a number of mergers, acquisitions and joint ventures unfolding over the next few years as the cannabis industry consolidates itself. This means that some of the upcoming businesses will be investing heavily in capital intensive projects in the early years with limited growth of capital.

However, this doesn't mean that you should exclude those businesses going through an initial growing pain cycle with limited revenues. Use this metric to help confirm the future profitability of the business.

Factor #2: Equity or Book Value per Share Growth Rate (BVPS).

The BVPS is what a business would be worth if it's no longer a business. This would be the liquidation value or book value of the company. The raw number is not important. It's the rate of equity growth that is key in comparing businesses. We're ultimately looking for businesses that are able to accumulate a growing surplus over time and not spending excessive funds to build new capital-intensive projects.

Expect the overall cannabis industry to experience sluggish growth of BVPS in the early stages of each business's degree of maturation. This is because most emerging market leaders are investing in capital-intensive projects.

Factor #3: Earnings per Share Growth Rate.

The EPS indicates how much the business is profiting per share of ownership. The EPS is often found as the last line on the income statement. However, we're more concerned with the growth rate, which we'll either quickly calculate on our own or find on certain financial websites that report business fundamentals. In general, a higher EPS indicates more value because investors are willing to pay more for a business with higher profits.

Factor #4: Sales or Revenue Growth Rate.

The sales growth rate represents the total dollars the business took in from selling its products and services. It's usually located on the top line of the income statement. This metric is the easiest to understand. Fundamentally, it serves as a key indicator as to how profitable the company is. Sales is what drives any business. An increasing revenue growth rate over time indicates that the business model is generating income.

Factor #5: Free Cash Flow Growth Rate.

Free cash flow is an indicator as to whether a business is growing its cash with profits or if the profits are only on paper. This value is the amount of cash which remains in the business after all expenditures have been paid. And since we're focusing our attention on growth rates, this metric should ideally be increasing year over year. This growth rate is a good indicator as to the overall health and financial well-being of the company.

Ideally, all of the growth rates should be equal to or greater than 10 percent per year for the last 5, 3 and 1 year(s). Having at least these three numbers gives you a better sense of how the company is growing over a period of time. Fundamental to all of the numbers is consistency. We want all the numbers going up or at least staying the same.

Factor #6: Debt-to-Equity Ratio.

The debt-to-equity ratio is a simple measure of how much the company owes in relation to how much it owns. It's calculated by dividing the total liabilities by the net equity. This ratio is easy to find on most financial websites. It should be low and preferably less than 0.5.

You can also look at a company's balance sheet to determine the total amount of debt coming due over the next few years. Here's a tip. Do a quick check is to see if the long-term debt of the company can be paid off in less than 3 years with the current free cash flow or net earnings. This gives you a margin of safety in assessing the extent of debt on the company's books. Ideally, this should be zero thus enabling the business to readily respond to drastic changes in the economy. However, those businesses capable of paying off debt within a 3-year window are still good prospects to consider.

Factor #7: PEG ratio.

A helpful indicator when comparing two or more like businesses together is the PEG ratio. The PEG is the Price-to-Earnings Multiple (P/E) divided by its earnings growth rate. It is an indicator of growth at a reasonable price, or what the stock investment industry calls GARP.

The PEG is a great way to identify growth stocks that are still selling at a good price. The lower the PEG the better, since you're getting more earnings growth for every dollar invested. As a rule of thumb, healthy companies have PEG rates less than 1, whereas a PEG rate over 2 is expensive.

The PEG ratio was championed by investment guru *Peter Lynch* who generated an annualized return of 29.8 % from 1977 to 1990 from Fidelity's Magellan Fund while the S&P 500 had an average return of 15.8 %.

Factor #8: Price-to-Sales Ratio.

The price-to-sales ratio was promoted by investment guru *Ken Fisher* back in the 80's. Fisher believed that earnings can be more volatile in the traditional P/E ratio as opposed to sales which tend to rarely decline in good companies. The PSR is calculated by dividing the stock price per share by the total sales per share. This ratio can help indicate if you're paying too much for the company's stock based on its sales. This is a useful indicator when assessing retailers in the cannabis market.

The general rule of thumb is that the lower the PSR the better. Cyclical retailers with a PSR between 0.4 and 0.8 are good investment candidates. A cyclical stock is one that does better when the economy is doing well, and people have more discretionary money to spend. The "recreational" cannabis market falls into this group. Noncyclical stocks with a PSR between 0.75 and 1.5 also offer good value for investors. The pharmaceutical industry falls into this category with "medical" marijuana producers being a part of this sector.

Factor #9: Relative Strength Index.

This is a technical indicator found on most stock charts. The RSI measures the velocity and magnitude of directional price movements in a stock. It's most typically used on a 14-day timeframe. The indicator is measured on a scale from 0 to 100, with high and low levels marked at 70 and 30, respectively.

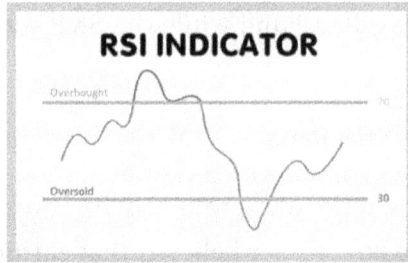

RSI Indicator

I've included this one technical indicator of stock momentum into the mix for screening potential candidates. The reason becomes apparent based on *James O'Shaughnessy* comment in his book *What Works on Wall Street* that:

> "we find that relative strength is among the only pure growth factors that actually beats the market consistently, by a wide margin."

Start your initial screening by looking for stocks that have an RSI above 50 and below 80 on a 100-point scale.

Please keep in mind that the cannabis industry is a relatively new one in terms of having an established, long, track record in the stock market. This means that many up-and-coming businesses do not have five years of financial data to base your "ideal" investment decisions on.

In this case, look for potential growth trends using the selection criteria mentioned. Companies entering into joint venture projects that'll increase overall market share are good bets.

Moving along to how 7 different types of economic moats help you make money in the markets.

Step 2 - Determine if the business is protected by an economic moat:

As you can see, there are many factors you could consider when choosing those top-notch businesses that have great growth potential and are capable of generating substantial profits for you over the years. So, how important is it that a company has a well-established economic moat? The short answer: crucial.

An economic moat refers to the notion that the business has some durable competitive advantage, not unlike a moat that protects a castle from attack. The wider the moat the easier it is to fend off attackers.

Finding a business with a wide moat is key to finding a successful business to own; the wider the moat, the more predictable its future 5 to 10 years down the road. Having a competitive edge, allows for a company to have a degree of predictability.

As an investor, you're looking for not only sustainable growth rates but also consistent growth in cash flow, equity and sales over a 3 to 5-year period of time. With increasing cash flow, profitability for both the business and you the shareholder arises. With increasing cash flow, a market leader can whether the ups and downs of the economic business cycle paying off debt when needed or investing capital for expanding into new markets. Wide moat companies are also protected from inflation since their "monopolistic position" enables them to raise prices at will.

Here are 5 types of economic moats to look for in a potential business that are geared specifically to the cannabis industry:

Moat #1: Brand – a product or service you're willing to pay more for because you know and trust it. Companies like Disney and Nike have good brand moats.

Moat #2: Secret - a patent, copyright or trade secret that makes competition difficult or illegal. Examples of these companies are 3M, Pfizer and Apple.

Moat #3: Toll - having exclusive control of a market through government approval or licensing thus being able to charge a "toll" for accessing that product or service. Such businesses as PG & E, a utility company and Warner Media fit the mold.

Moat #4: Low Price - products priced so low no one can compete because they enjoy massive economies of scale due to a huge market share. Home Depot, Costco and Wal-Mart are examples of businesses that have used pricing to establish an economic advantage.

Moat #5: Network Effect - the ability to quickly dominate a network of end-users by being first in the market. eBay was the first online auction business to dominate the North American market.

You need not find a company with multiple moats to consider it to be a potential investment candidate. It should have one moat that seems hardest to cross and one that is sustainable long-term.

The establishment of a viable economic moat shows up in the fundamentals. Companies with consistently high growth rates of over 10% per year in return on invested capital, sales, equity and free cash over many years are the ideal candidates.

Unfortunately, for the most part businesses operating within the cannabis industry do not benefit from a durable competitive advantage or economic moat. That's not to say that an innovator may come along and create such an advantage in the processing and product development arenas.

Right now, look for cannabis stocks that show signs of being able to tap into one of the five types of economic moats. It could be a proprietary technology, ultra-low-cost production facility, patented pharmaceutical, or exclusive distribution agreement. These are the players that have the potential to outpace the rest of the market.

As previously mentioned, cannabis is destined to become commoditized. This won't happen in the short-term, but it will occur as the global marketplace opens up in the next few years. Seeking players in the international arena that have factored commoditization into their business model, allows you to better position yourself for the long haul and profit from early investments destined to grow significantly.

Step 3 - Assess if management is on your side?

Let's take a look at who is running the company. As obvious as it may be, we want management to be on the side of the shareholder. However, this is not always the case.

The stock market has seen countless cases of incidents where the CEO did not have the shareholder's best interest at heart. Situations where the CEO is being paid hundreds of millions of dollars to run the company into the ground.

Here are the top four qualities that you want to see in great CEO's:

1. They are service-oriented as opposed to ego-oriented.

Their focus is on serving the owners, the employees, the suppliers, and the customers.

2. They are passionate about their work and the business they are managing.
3. They never risk their honor to make a quick buck or ruin their reputation for power or prestige.
4. They are driven to change the world for the better. They have big goals that inspire and motivate the organization.

The question now becomes, how do you go about finding this information?

Here are three ways to check out the management team without hiring a private eye:

1. Google the CEO's name and read a few news articles in trade and business magazines and newspapers, such as Forbes, Fortune, Barron's, Success, the New York Times and the Wall Street Journal. What reputation does the CEO have in the business community?
2. Read the CEO's letter to shareholders and compare the growth rate numbers to what is being said. What is the tone of the letter? Look for CEO's who take responsibility for a bad year, as evidenced in the numbers, admits his or her mistakes and tells shareholders what he or she intends to do. These CEO's have integrity.
3. Look at the Insider trading activity on MSN Money, Yahoo Finance, or possibly your broker's website. If company executives are unloading more than 30 percent of their stock all at once, this is not a good sign. As well, look for CEO's that are getting overpaid through stock options or

outrageous perks in addition to their salary. Most free websites post this basic data.

Ask yourself, does the business have great management? You must be confident that the people running the business are doing so as if they intend on being there for decades and not out to rip you off in the short term. Does that make sense?

Once you've explored a business's fundamentals, competitive advantage and management team you can use the same approach with that business's key competitors to determine who is the market leader in the cannabis industry.

By identifying and investing initially in only these best-of-breed companies, especially when they come on sale at attractive prices, you increase the likelihood that you'll build a successful investment portfolio.

Holy Moses Randall, how the heck am I to keep track of all this info? Great question, my wannabe investor.

All of this information can be recorded either in a notebook or in an Excel Spreadsheet. Although taking a little more time to set up, a spreadsheet affords the greatest future ease of use for both the calculations and updating information. This process has served me well in assessing potential candidates. It has helped me streamline the information flow so that I am more efficient, saving me time in the process.

Staying organized with charts and tables provides you with a quick snapshot of those businesses to keep your eye on.

As well, your broker may provide you with a simple system for keeping track of certain stocks placed on your watchlist.

Who is the main competitor in the cannabis industry?

Most analysts feel that the biggest competitor facing the cannabis industry right now is the illicit cannabis market. The transition from the illicit market to the regulated market is occurring at different rates in different jurisdictions, but the trend is clear. The vast majority of cannabis consumers prefer using product that is legal and tested to be free of pesticides and other toxins.

Unlike other high growth industries, there is already a massive market of people using cannabis. As well, the size of the pie itself is growing. New consumers are flocking to the industry, especially in jurisdictions providing consumers with a legal source of cannabis-related products.

Unfortunately, it takes time for the legalization process to unfold as many levels of government are involved in the vetting process, the creation of laws and bi-laws, as well as establishing product quality control, distribution and marketing guidelines and rules.

This has led to supply and demand challenges. For example, in 2019 most Canadian jurisdictions could not provide enough legal outlets for recreational cannabis users to access, which has ended up fostering the growth of the underground industry.

As easy access to a variety of recreational and medicinal products improves, so will corporate revenues as consumers shift from the underground market to legitimate retailers capable of offering a greater variety of quality products.

～

9

SELECTING INVESTMENT STRATEGIES

Before we take a look at one specific time-tested strategy outlined in this audiobook, let's take a quick look at the obvious challenge many retail investors are faced with - that of picking which strategy to use.

With so many popular investment strategies in the stock market, it can be a bit daunting and overwhelming trying to select the one's that consistently accelerate the velocity of your money.

Many experts tout that they have the perfect strategy that is the be-all and end-all to solving your investment woes. Many well-known investment authors who have been successful investing in the stock market often have a strong bias towards a particular strategy that better sells their services or investment product lines.

It's challenging to get an unbiased opinion about any particular investment strategy. Who can you really trust when many of them have a hidden agenda? The American Association of Individual

Investors currently tracks over 60 investment strategies on their website. It's no wonder that most do-it-yourself retail investors are at a loss as to which approach to take. Fortunately, there is a simple plan of attack.

The most important aspect about making money in the markets is to stick to a proven strategy over time. It becomes more of a factor the longer you work your specific strategy through good times and bad. Avoid adopting the attitude that if Plan A fails, you've got 25 more letters to choose from.

Trading momentum stocks strategy:

This resource focuses on providing you with a handful of investment strategies that will accelerate your wealth generation in the stock market. One strategy to consider placing in your arsenal, is investing in momentum stocks. This is also known as using a trend-following approach to investing.

With a trend-following strategy, you only invest in stocks when they're rising, selling them immediately as they begin to fall below a certain threshold level. With this strategy, there's no need to predict the future. Only the price action of the stock tells you what you should be doing. Using this strategy limits your need to use multiple indicators, charts or news feeds, simplifying the investment process.

Trading momentum is best done with young companies that are rapidly growing their sales. And guess what? Most cannabis businesses fall into this category. Sweet!

Well-established, mature companies that often pay a dividend are not good momentum stock plays. They tend to be slow-growing. To entice investors to park their money in these steady, slow growers, these "blue chip" stocks reward these patient investors with quarterly dividends.

Fast-growing stocks tend to be more volatile as future earnings are difficult to predict. Money can flow into and out of these stocks in great waves. We want to catch the upside momentum of these stocks so that we can take advantage of the accelerated revenue growth. This approach works well with an accelerated cash flow investment system, just like pizza and beer - two of the main food categories of college students and cannabis producers.

To quickly screen for these momentum plays, we'll look at two main criteria - one fundamental indicator and the other technical (i.e. stock chart):

1. Annual revenue growth rate >15%. (fundamental)
2. 50-day moving average > 200-day average. (technical)

Ideally, we would like to see the revenue (sales) growth rate above 15% for a 3-year period of time. Many cannabis stocks will meet this minimum criterion by 2021.

A buy signal for a momentum stock would be triggered when the stock's 50-day moving average crosses above its 200-day moving average and the stock is currently trading above its 50-day moving average. This information can be found by looking at a technical chart of the stock, which you can access through your online brokerage account. This is often the default setting for many technical charts.

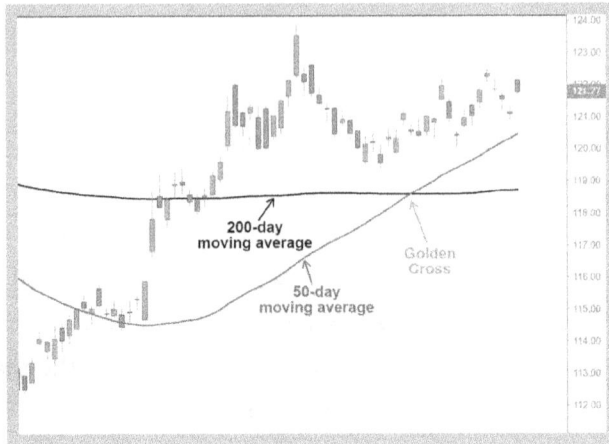

Assessing Moving Averages

Using a momentum strategy, you would purchase the stock at this point and ride the trend for as long as you can until you've reached a point where you've realized a 300% gain. Setting things up is the easy part. The hurry up and wait patiently part is a bit more challenging.

As for exiting your position, there are three signals to keep an eye on:

1. **If the stock drops 15% from your purchase price.** This prevents any potential losses from becoming too big. Using a wide stop-loss allows for wider swings in the market with these potentially volatile stocks. By setting a narrow stop-loss of say 5%, you may be taken out of the market due to the natural volatility in the markets that particular day.

2. **If the 50-day moving average closes below the 200-day, sell the stock.** The trend is now over, and momentum could be moving in a negative direction. After a long

trend has occurred, this is the signal to exit and take any profits off the table.

3. **If the stock rises 300% from your purchase price, sell the stock.** Exit the stock completely and take your profits. You've benefitted from a significant rise in the stock price. Now it's time to look for the next best momentum play.

As a side note, to quickly calculate what a 300% yippee kay yay exit price would be for any stock, simply multiply the initial stock price by 4. Voila! Done.

As you can surmise, the assumption being made is that you'll risk 15% in order to make 300%. In essence, one winning trade will pay for 20 losing trades. That's a super risk-reward ratio. Even if you have to exit your positions 90% of the time, you still can expect to average over 15% over the long term with your portfolio. Not a bad return, wouldn't you surmise?

The question now becomes: How much capital should I risk for each trade?

Investment gurus are all over the map on this one. Most keep their trades small, as small as 2% of their overall portfolio value. This approach reduces portfolio risk significantly.

As a basic rule of thumb, you shouldn't invest more than 15% in any given position. Nor should you risk more than you're comfortably prepared to lose because any position can quickly head south on you.

Let's put this all into perspective with a simplified example. We'll assume that you have a total of $15,000 in your trading accounts. If you're just starting out, it may make sense to spread out your stock acquisitions over 15 picks. This would mean allocating up to $1000 for each buy signal. If one of your stocks should drop 15%, forcing you to exit your position, you would lose $150 from the trade or 1% of your trading portfolio. Even when you factor in transaction fees, this is a manageable loss. It's not as if you're going to have to sell the house and move back into your parent's basement should this scenario pan out.

It's important to remember that when you adopt a momentum trading strategy that you will incur losses. Mitigating your losses with an appropriate allocation strategy becomes paramount to your success. By focusing on stocks with high revenue growth and following the three exit signals previously discussed, you increase the probability of coming out on top with your stock picks.

When you use this particular buy-sell momentum strategy, you're not only profiting from rapid risers but you're also in a position to side-step bear (down) markets. The 50-day and 200-day moving averages can be used with the major stock indices to help predict when a downturn in the markets can be anticipated.

Just as with individual stocks, when the 50-day moving average crosses below the 200-day moving average this indicates that the market's upward momentum is slowing or even reversing. It may be time to consider exiting your positions, especially if revenue growth stalls. Just patiently sit in cash until the next growth opportunity presents itself.

10

TIMING ENTERING & EXITING POSITIONS?

Contrary to what many in the investment landscape are saying about timing the market, you can learn to be more adept at moving into and out of positions so that you increase the probability of coming out on top.

One of the most frustrating aspects of stock investing is trying to figure out when you should move into and out of positions. It can take you years to figure out what time periods you should avoid based on the documented historical trends.

It can also take the average investor years to figure out how the movement of the big institutional players affects one's ability to profit from the entry and exit points in the market.

You will in all likelihood NOT be able to time the market tops and bottoms, thus enabling you to maximize your profits. No one has been able to consistently do this in the stock market.

However, we can take advantage of certain times of the day, week, month or year that enable us to better optimize our profits. This knowledge helps you create your "edge" thereby increasing your profitability potential in the stock market.

Seven timing tips to generating better returns:

The following are my top seven tips to better timing the market and more importantly why.

Tip #1: Avoid buying stock or call options on a Monday.

If you decide to move into a position on Monday morning, expect higher than normal price volatility throughout the day.

According to former trading floor boss *Joe Terranova* in his book *Buy High Sell Higher*:

> *"Whether traders love or hate their personal lives, the pros that move the market often come into the office on Mondays in a bad mood. Whatever the reason, there is always a flood of emotion coursing through the market on Mondays. Markets that are trading on emotions are not where you want to be. I make a point of never trading on Mondays."*

I tend to concur with Joe. You as a cash flow investor are better served by waiting for the markets to play out during the course of the day on Mondays. They tend to be too emotionally charged after the weekend.

Tip #2: Try to trade on Wednesdays and Thursdays. Be cautious of Fridays.

On the flip side of the coin is to ask yourself when would be the ideal time to try to better time my market plays? Mid-week tends to present better investment opportunities than either the beginning or end of the week. According to *Jeffrey Hirsch* in his book the *Stock Trader's Almanac* Wednesday's have produced the most gains since 1990.

Often on Fridays many big institutional players unload certain positions before the weekend, preferring not to hold potentially volatile stocks that may be affected by news over the weekend. This coupled with the notion that many traders take off early on Friday afternoon means that the smaller players become the temporary price movers. Watch to see that the price movement of the stock is in synch with the volume of shares being traded. A rising stock price yet decreasing volume is a signal that the current stock price trend is unsustainable over time.

Tip #3: Avoid trading first thing in the morning and during the lunch hour.

As to what time of the day may present better buy and sell opportunities, consider waiting at least an hour or so after the opening bell before getting into the market. I've made this mistake a couple of times, only to realize later in the morning that I overpaid for my positions. Another time of the day that may be problematic is midday during the Eastern time zone lunch hour when many professional traders take their lunch. With fewer traders, market volume tends to lag.

A little patience as to seeing how the day may be unfolding may save you a few bucks in the end. By waiting until the end of the day when volume is typically the heaviest, you may be in a better position to assess your timing opportunity. Remember that above average volume with rising stock prices is a signal that investors are confident in a particular stock or the market as a whole.

Tip #4: Avoid trading at the end or beginning of a quarter.

Be very attentive as to stocks that you may be holding which have been lack luster over the past quarter. Many institutional players unload poor performers in an attempt to re-balance their overall portfolio. Keep in mind that the mutual fund industry is very competitive with many fund managers taking a short-term approach to investing in order to hang onto their client's money.

By being vigilant at the end of each quarter you can better assess the impact of buying or selling particular holdings based on what you feel the big boys may be doing. Sometimes you can get a feel for the tone of the market as a whole by watching how money is flowing into the stock market as opposed to the bond market or commodities such as gold and oil.

Tip #5: Avoid trading when company earnings are announced.

The time period just leading up to and soon after an earnings report release can see volatile stock price movement. Earnings reports can signal shifts in momentum. This is especially important when you'll be selling covered calls on the stock during the same month that earnings are going to be announced.

Err on the side of caution. Wait out the period around the earnings report release to see how Mr. Market will handle the information rather than commit yourself to a call position. You can always take up a position once you're assured that the news will not have a negative effect on your positions.

Tip #6: Be wary of the first 2 to 3 weeks of January.

Many companies have year-end earnings announcements in January, which can translate into increased stock price volatility.

The large institutional players typically have major capital allocation flows in and out of stocks during this period of time. This is especially so with the commodity-based funds. If you've identified a commodity-based stock that you would like to invest in, you may be better served waiting on the sidelines until the big boys have finished their dance with increased price volatility. Since cannabis is destined to be a commodity-based industry, be wary of this time period moving forward.

I'm guilty of making this mistake. Instead of being more patient with purchasing a particular stock, I ended up initially paying more for the investment as the stock dropped in price mid-January. I had to wait on the sidelines for a short period of time until April for the stock to appreciate up to a level that I felt comfortable selling option contracts at.

As you know, the name of the game is increasing the velocity of your money. Unfortunately, my money was parked in a position whereby I was unable to generate a monthly cash flow.

Tip #7: Schedule any important moves after mid-April.

The stock market tends to be more prone to weakness after the mid-month tax deadline in the United States. This may be the result of individual investor money moving out of the markets in order to pay for tax obligations owing and the rebalancing of portfolios in order take advantage of certain capital losses.

For your own personal finances, you may wish to hold off any major moves that could have an impact on your current tax liabilities owing. It may be prudent to check with a financial planner or accountant prior to making any such big moves.

Exit strategies: Seven times to sell your stock.

There are many compelling reasons as to why you "could' sell one of your holdings. However, there are few reasons that justify why you really "should" cash out of your position. So, when is an "appropriate" time to sell a stock?

Consider these top 7 reasons why you might close out a position:

Reason #1: Exceptional Stock Growth.

Consider cashing out when your stock has done well and appreciated above your target price, for example having realized a 300% growth in the appreciation of the stock price when using a momentum strategy. Time to take some money off of the table and look for the next winning investment.

Reason #2: Poor Business.

If the company fundamentals have changed for the worse and the stock is tanking, you're better off quickly cutting your losses and repositioning your capital. Remember we don't want dead money sitting around. Get out and get into something that has a higher probability of generating better returns. Exiting when you've lost no more than 15% of your equity may be a prudent rule to follow.

Reason #3: Can't Sleep.

When you've reached your risk tolerance level and your holding is keeping you up at night, it may be time to liquidate your position and re-evaluate your investment portfolio. I did this with an options play that I was uncomfortable with from the get-go.

Despite taking a loss, I was able to sleep better, refocus my energy and find a better opportunity that I was very happy to be in.

Reason #4: Reached Your Goal.

It would be appropriate to move your capital when you've achieved a specific financial goal in the markets and would like to buy a house, fund a college education or build a business.

Reason #5: Opportunity Knocks.

At times, you may need the cash for another investment opportunity such as rental real estate, a systematized business or an angel capital investment. Remember that your focus is on accelerating the velocity of your money from one great opportunity to a better one. Keep an open mind to any and all future possibilities that get you closer to realizing your dreams that much faster.

Reason #6: Retirement.

Should you be in the enviable position to retire, you may wish to shift some of your capital into other assets during retirement or use some of your capital to periodically fund part of your retirement. Doing so with capital coming from a tax-free account makes it even more rewarding.

Reason #7: Unexpected Expense.

As a last resort. you may be faced with an unexpected medical bill or emergency that requires you to liquidate your stock holding. Not an ideal situation to be faced with, but nevertheless an appropriate one should it arise out of the spur of the moment.

Now, that you've explored various entry and exit strategy parameters, let's take a look at your daily routine when it comes to investing.

Ideally, you'll want to check on your positions twice a day. Taking 10 - 15 minutes in the morning and at the end of the day should keep you abreast of what is happening in the market and hopefully keep you out of any serious trouble.

First things first. After you've had your green drink smoothie, tall glass of water or cup of java in the morning, log into your online broker account. Ah coffee! The sweet balm by which many of us accomplish tasks. Sorry, I digress.

You could also check out how the overall markets are doing at websites such as FinViz or Yahoo Finance.

Step #1: Take a moment to review your trading rules and/or those in this resource. This will allow you to more fully focus your attention on making the best decisions that move your investment portfolio forward.

Step #2: Review the overall market sentiment and any global news that may directly affect your current holdings.

Step #3: Review the news for each stock that you're holding. If the news is positive, think about how you could capture any gains. And if the news is negative, consider an appropriate exit strategy, if need be. Also check each stock's technical chart to verify if there were any gaps overnight that could affect your current strategy. A gap is a rapid decrease or increase in stock appreciation over a short period of time caused by high volume movement of the stock in one direction.

Step #4: Take any appropriate action, if need be.

Step #5: Towards the end of the trading day around 3:30 PM EST, review the news to see if there is anything negative that might affect your positions. If you're unable to do so right before the markets close, at least verify how your holdings are doing later that evening.

Step #6: Take a quick look at a technical chart for each stock to make sure that they're behaving according to your trading plan.

Step #7: Take any appropriate action, if need be. Depending on what the situation is, you may wish to wait a day or so to see if it resolves itself.

Keep in mind that once you develop an efficient habit for checking on each of your positions, your time commitment will be minimal.

Here are some closing thoughts.

The choice is yours right now. You can let life happen to you. Or you can embrace the wealth of insights, advice and strategies in this book and begin building life on your terms.

You've been armed with a number of investment strategies that work together to quickly accelerate the velocity of your money. The F.A.S.T. approach described in this guide provides you with the structural framework from which to build each of your positions.

In essence, this step-by-step guide walks you through the key steps to finding, assessing, strategizing and timing those big market plays in the cannabis industry. Should you like to explore stock investing approaches in greater detail, please check out the following free resources:

Stock Investing Tool Kit

How to Get $29 Worth of Investment Research for Free

Free Bonus #1: Top 5 Current Stock Market Trends.

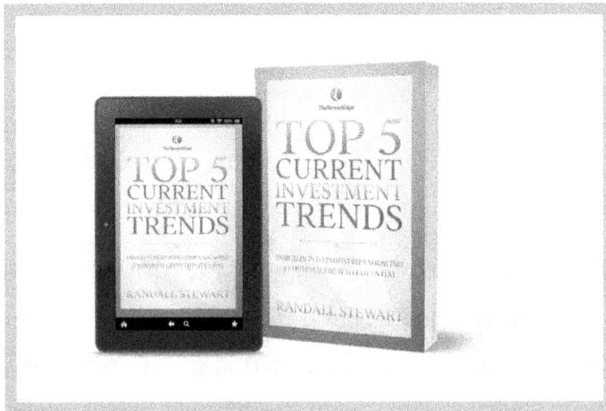

Tap into 5 industries poised to show consistent growth over the next two years. Take advantage of changes in the economic climate that'll fuel rapid growth in certain sectors.

Free Bonus #2: Growth Investing using the C.A.N.S.L.I.M. Approach.

Find market leaders using the key insights from the C.A.N.S.L.I.M. approach to growth investing. Quickly implement the main strategies summarized in this special report.

Free Bonus #3: Momentum Stock Investing Guidelines.

Guide your decision-making with a series of actionable rules and a trading routine that'll allow you to increase your probability of coming out on top. Learn how to optimize your returns in fast-growing stocks.

To receive your stock investing tool kit and discover how to capture the upside momentum of fast-growing market leaders, go to:

http://tiny.cc/stock-investing

I'm reminded of the question as to when the best time would be to plant a tree. The best time is 20 years ago. The second-best time is right now. I hope that you choose to act today and begin increasing the velocity of your money in the stock market. Imagine where you might be 5 years from now If you mastered some of these skills, especially with an industry destined to grow globally by leaps and bounds.

Ready to get started? I'm sure you are. To your ongoing success.

36 RESOURCES TO EXPLORE

Here is a list of the majority of the resources that I've used over the years to help me become a better investor. Some of these are classic guides that have stood the test of time. Should something tickle your fancy, check out those topics that may be of interest.

A Random Walk Down Wall Street: The Time-Tested Strategy for Successful Investing
Burton Malkiel
Publisher: W. W. Norton & Company (2020)
Paperback: 480 pages

All About Market Indicators: The Easy Way to Get Started
Michael Sincere
Publisher: McGraw Hill (2011)
Paperback: 217 pages

Beating the Street:

Peter Lynch
Publisher: Simon & Schuster (1993)
Hardcover: 318 pages

Buy and Hedge: The 5 Iron Rules for Investing Over the
Long Term
Jay Pestrichelli & Wayne Ferbert
Publisher: FT Press (2012)
Hardcover: 289 pages

Buy High Sell Higher: Why Buy-AND-Hold Is Dead & Other
Investing Lessons from CNBC's "The Liquidator"
Joe Terranova
Publisher: Business Plus (2012)
Hardcover: 261 pages

Cashing in on Covered Calls
Alan Ellman
Publisher: SAMR Productions (2007)
Paperback: 392 pages

Covered Calls Beginner's Guide
Randall Stewart
Publisher: Stewart Edge Publishing (2020)
Paperback: 198 pages

DNA of Success
Jack Zufelt
Publisher: Z Publishing (2003)
Paperback: 208 pages

Exit Strategies for Covered Calls
Alan Ellman
Publisher: Wheatmark (2009)
Paperback: 178 pages

Getting Back to Even: Your Personal Economic Recovery Plan
James J. Cramer
Publisher: Simon & Schuster (2009)
Hardcover: 352 pages

Getting Started in Options
Michael Thomsett
Publisher: John Wiley & Sons (2007)
Paperback: 383 pages

High Probability Trading
Marcel Link
Publisher: McGraw Hill (2003)
Hardcover: 393 pages

How to Make Money in Stocks
William O'Neil
Publisher: McGraw Hill (2009)
Paperback: 464 pages

Intelligent Investor: The Definitive Book on Value Investing by
Benjamin Graham, et al.
Publisher: Harper Business (2006)
Paperback: 640 pages

Little Book of Big Dividends: A Safe Formula for Guaranteed
Returns
Charles B. Carlson
Publisher: John Wiley & Sons (2010)
Hardcover: 174 pages

Little Book of Common Sense Investing
John Bogle
Publisher: Wiley (2017)
Paperback: 304 pages

Market Mind Games
Denise Shull
Publisher: McGraw-Hill (2011)
Hardcover: 288 pages

Millionaire Fastlane
MJ DeMarco
Publisher: Viperion (2011)
Paperback: 322 pages

Millionaire Maker: Act, Think, and Make Money the Way the
Wealthy Do
Loral Langemeier
Publisher: McGraw-Hill (2005)
Hardcover: 240 pages

Millionaire Next Door: The Surprising Secrets of America's
Wealthy
Thomas Stanley & William Danko
Publisher: Taylor Trade Publishing (2010)

Paperback: 272 pages

Money Girl's Smart Moves to Grow Rich (Quick & Dirty Tips)
Laura Adams
Publisher: St. Martin's Griffin (2010)
Paperback: 254 pages

New Insights on Covered Call Writing
Richard Lehman & Lawrence McMillan
Publisher: Bloomberg Press (2003)
Hardcover: 240 pages

Options Made Easy: Your Guide to Profitable Trading
Guy Cohen
Publisher: FT Press (2005)
Hardcover: 335 pages

Options Trading for the Conservative Investor: Increasing Profits
without Increasing Risk
Michael C. Thomsett
Publisher: Prentice Hall (2005)
Paperback: 255 pages

Power Curve
Scott Kyle
Publisher: Nautilus Press (2009)
Hardcover: 256 pages

Power of Focus
Jack Canfield, Mark Victor Hansen and Les Hewitt
Publisher: HCI (2000)

Paperback: 310 pages

Rich Dad's Guide to Investing
Robert Kiyosaki
Publisher: Time Warner Books (2000)
Paperback: 403 pages

Rule #1: The Simple Strategy for Successful Investing in Only 15 Minutes a Week
Phil Town
Publisher: Three Rivers Press (2007)
Paperback: 330 pages

Secrets of the Millionaire Mind
T. Harv Eker
Publisher: Harper Business (2005)
Hardcover: 224 pages

Stock Trader's Almanac
Jeffrey Hirsch & Yale Hirsch
Publisher: John Wiley & Sons
Hardcover: 192 pages

Succeed: How We Can Reach Our Goals
Dr. Heidi Grant Halverson
Publisher: Hudson Street Press (2010)
Hardcover: 288 pages

Trade Like a Stock Market Wizard
Mark Minervini
Publisher: McGraw-Hill Education (2013)

Hardcover: 352 pages

Trading in the Zone
Mark Douglas
Publisher: Prentice Hall Press (2001)
Hardcover: 240 pages

Unfair Advantage: The Power of Financial Education
Robert Kiyosaki
Publisher: Plata Publishing (2011)
Paperback: 275 pages

Ultimate Dividend Playbook
Josh Peters
Publisher: John Wiley & Sons (2008)
Hardcover: 352 pages

What Works on Wall Street: The Classic Guide to the Best-
Performing Investment Strategies of All Time
James P. O'Shaughnessy
Publisher: McGraw Hill (2012)
Hardcover: 681 pages